APPLE W.
USER GUIDE

**A Complete User Manual with Step
By Step Instruction For Beginners
And Seniors To Learn How To Use
The Apple Watch Series 9 Like A Pro
With WatchOS 10 Tips & Tricks**

BY

HERBERT A. CLARK

Table of Contents

INTRODUCTION

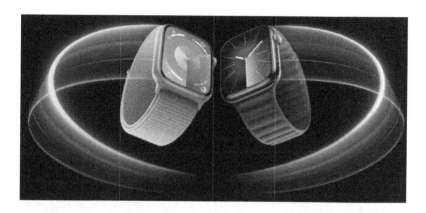

Welcome to Apple Watch Series 9, the versatile wrist companion that can help you to be more active, track health data, & most importantly stay connected with people you care about—with or without your iPhone.

This step-by-step manual will help you find all the great things the Apple Watch Series 9 can do.

What's in the Box

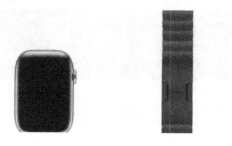

FEATURES OF APPLE WATCH SERIES 9

Design

The new Apple Watch did not receive a design update. It still has the same rounded, square look like the previous generation, and it's available in 41 mm & 45 mm size options.

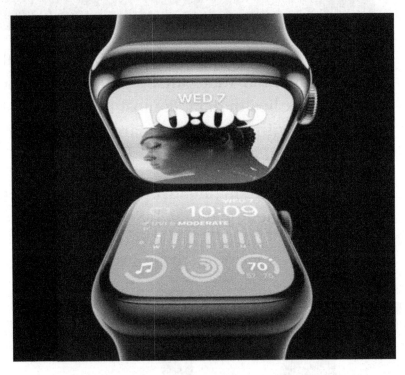

The Apple Watch has smooth, rounded edges around the screen and weighs between 32g and 51.5g, depending on the size and material of the case.

The new watch has a black ceramic & crystal back which houses 4 photodiodes & 4 LED clusters to make it easy for health-monitoring features like ECG & blood oxygen monitoring to function properly.

There's a Digital Crown on the watch's side which can be used for navigation & scrolling, and a side button that can be used to confirm Apple Pay purchases, access emergency services, etc.

Colours & materials

The new Apple Watch is available in stainless steel & aluminum. The aluminum model is the cheapest, while the stainless steel models are more expensive.

The aluminum model comes in (PRODUCT) RED, Pink, Silver, Starlight, & Midnight colour options. While, the Stainless steel model comes in Space Black, Graphite, Gold, & Silver colour options.

41 mm

- ❖ Stainless steel: 42.30g
- ❖ Aluminum: 31.9g

45 mm

- ❖ Stainless steel: 51.50g
- ❖ Aluminum: 38.7g

Water & dust resistance

The smartwatch features IP6X dust resistance for use in places like the beach, & WR50 water resistance, rated for water immersion as deep as 50m.

Since it is rated for 50m of water immersion, the Apple Watch Series 9 can be used in the ocean or a swimming pool. It is only suitable for shallow water activity and cannot be used for waterskiing, scuba diving, or other activities that involve high-speed water or deep water submersion.

Double Tap Gesture

You can now use the Double Tap gesture to control your smartwatch. When you double-tap your thumb & index finger, your watch's sensor detects the movement and activates what is on your screen, allowing you to do things like start or stop a timer, pause or play songs, open notifications, end calls, answer calls, etc.

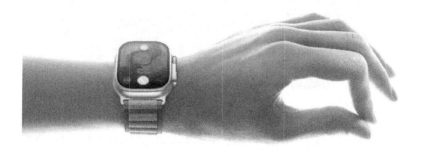

Storage

The new smartwatch has 64 GB of storage space

Crash Detection

If your smartwatch detects a serious car accident, it can help you contact emergency services and alert your emergency contacts.

When your smartwatch notices a serious car accident, it'll show an alert & automatically begin an emergency call after twenty seconds unless you cancel. If you're unresponsive, your watch will send a voice message to the emergency department, telling them that you have been involved in a serious car accident. It will also send your location details to emergency services.

Health Features

The new Apple Watch offers health monitoring features like a 3rd-gen optical heart-rate sensor that calculates metrics such as a high heart-rate, resting heart-rate, & calories burned. You can also use the electric heart rate sensor to take an ECG, while the infrared light & LEDs allow users to track blood oxygen level. An inbuilt gyroscope & accelerometer allows other important health-related features like Fall detection to function properly.

Your smartwatch can detect irregular, high & low heart rates. It can also detect health issues like AFib & send you notifications when it detects anomalies.

Battery life

The Watch Series **9** offers an "all-day" 18-hour battery life from a single charge, which can be increased to about 36 hours with the Low Power Mode.

SETUP YOUR APPLE WATCH

Before setting up your Apple Watch you need to update your iPhone to the latest version of iOS, activate Bluetooth & connect your iPhone to a cellular or WiFi network.

Switch on your watch and wear it

Hold down the side button till the Apple symbol appears on your display. Then wear your smartwatch on your wrist.

Bring your smartwatch near your iPhone

When the **"Use iPhone to setup Apple Watch"** notification pops up on your phone screen, click on **Continue**. If you did not see this message on your screen, head over to the Watch application on your phone, touch the **All Watches** button, and then click on **Add Watch**.

If this is your own watch, click on the **Setup For Myself** button.

Ensure your smartwatch & iPhone are near each other while you follow these steps.

Scan the animation

Set your phone in a way that the watch face can be seen in the view finder. Wait to see an alert stating that your smartwatch has been connected to your phone.

If you cannot make use of the camera, or the animation does not appear, or your phone cannot read it, click on **Pair Manually**, and then follow the instructions.

Setup as new or restore from backup

If this is your first Apple smartwatch, click on the **Setup as New Apple Watch** button. If prompted, update your watch to the latest watchOS version.

If you have paired another Apple smartwatch with your current phone before, you'll see a screen that says "**Make This Your New Watch**". Click on App & Data and Settings to see how Express Set up is going to configure your new smartwatch. Then click on the **Continue** button. Click on the **Customize Setting** option if you want to choose how your new smartwatch will be configured. Then pick one of the backups from another previous Apple Watch to restore. Or, if you want to fully personalize your smartwatch's settings, touch the **Setup as New Apple Watch** option.

Select the wrist you want to put on your smartwatch and then click on **Continue**.

Go through the Terms & Conditions and then click on **Agree**.

Log in with your Apple ID

If prompted, type your Apple ID passcode. If you're not asked, you can login any time from the Watch application: Click on the **General** button> Apple ID, and then log in

If the Find My feature is not setup on your phone, you will be prompted to activate **Activation Lock**. If you enter the Activation Lock screen, it means that your smartwatch is already linked to an Apple ID. You'll need to insert the Apple ID's details to continue setup.

Create a login code

You can decide to skip this part, but you will need a passcode if you want to use features like Apple Pay on your smartwatch.

On your phone, click on the **Create Pass code** button or the **Add Long Pass-code** button, and then type the new passcode on your watch. To skip this part, click on the **Don't Add Passcode** option.

Personalize your settings

Choose your desired text size.

If you did not make use of Express Set up, your smartwatch will show you the settings it shares with your Phone. If you enable features like Location Service, Diagnostics, Find My, & WiFi Calling for your Phone, these settings will automatically activate on your smartwatch.

Next, add or update info like your birthdate to ensure your Health & Fitness data are correct. You can also enable health notifications like noise level, & more.

Setup cellular & Apple Pay

You can setup cellular if your smartwatch is a cellular model.

Next, you will be prompted to setup Apple Pay by adding cards. Then your phone will walk you through features such as Always On Display and your preferred application view.

Allow your devices to synchronize

Your smartwatch will display the watch face when the pairing process has been completed. Keep your phone near your smartwatch so that both devices can keep synchronizing info in the background

Unpair your smartwatch

❖ Launch the Watch application on your phone.
❖ Click on the **My Watch** button, and then click on the **All Watches** button.

❖ Touch the Information icon ⓘ beside the Apple Watch, and then click on the **Unpair Apple Watch** button.

Pair more than one watch

You can connect another Apple smartwatch the same way you connected the first one. Or adhere to the directives below:

❖ Launch the Watch application.
❖ Click on the **My Watch** button, and then click on the **All Watches** button.

❖ Click on the **Add Watch** option, and then adhere to the directives on your display.

Quickly switch to another Apple smartwatch

Your smartphone will detect the paired Apple Watch you are putting on & automatically connect to it. Simply wear another Apple Watch & lift your hand.

You can also select an Apple smartwatch manually:

❖ Launch the Watch application.
❖ Click on the **My Watch** button, and then click on the **All Watches** button.
❖ Deactivate Auto-Switch

To know if your smartwatch is connected to your phone, long-press your watch's side button to reveal the Controls Center, and then look for the

Connection Status logo

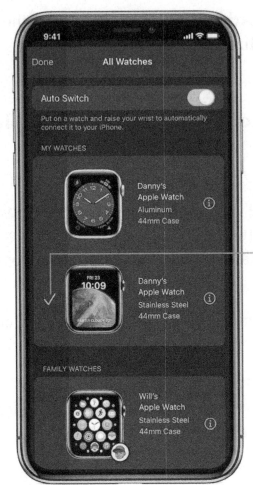

The active Apple Watch.

BASICS

Apple Watch

The following images would help you get started with using the Apple Watch Series 9

Display

Digital Crown

Microphone

Side button

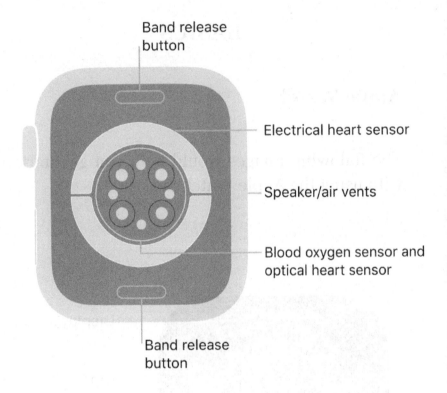

Band release
button

Electrical heart sensor

Speaker/air vents

Blood oxygen sensor and
optical heart sensor

Band release
button

Apple Watch gestures

Use the following gestures to interact with your smartwatch.

❖ Tap: Use a finger to gently touch your display.

❖ Swipe: Move one of your fingers across your display—right, left, down, or up.

❖ Drag: Swipe across your display without lifting your finger.

Apple Watch app

You can use the Watch application on your iPhone to personalize watch faces, customize settings & notifications, customize the Dock, install applications, etc.

Adhere to the directives below to open the Watch application:

* Touch the Watch application icon on your iPhone
* Touch the **My Watch** tab to view your Apple Watch settings

Swipe to see your watch face collection.

Settings for Apple Watch.

Switch your smartwatch on & off

❖ Switch on: To switch on your device, simply hold down the side button till you see the Apple symbol on the screen (you may see a black screen at first).

A watch face will appear when your Smartwatch is on.

❖ Switch off: Hold down the side button till you see the slider on your screen, touch the Power button ⏻ on the upper right, and then drag the Power Off slider to the right edge of your screen.

You can check the time when your smartwatch is switched off, to do this, simply long-press the Digital Crown.

Note: You cannot switch off your smartwatch when it's connected to power. You have to first remove it from the charger before you can switch it off.

Charge your smartwatch

Setup the charger

❖ Put the charging cable or charger on a flat surface in a well-ventilated space.

The Apple Watch Series 9 comes with a Magnetic Fast Charger to USB-C cable.

❖ Connect the charging cable to the power adapter.
❖ Connect the adapter to the power outlet.

Start charging

Put the Magnetic charger or charging cable on the back of your smartwatch. The concave end of the charger will snap to the back of your smartwatch & align neatly.

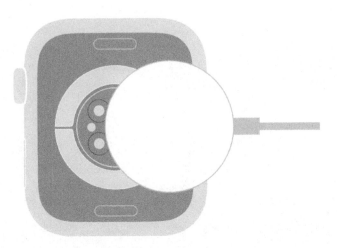

Your smartwatch will play a chime when it starts charging (unless it's in silent mode) & display a charge icon ⚡ on the watch face. The icon turns red when the battery is low, and turns green when it's connected to power.

You can also charge your smartwatch in a flat position or on its side.

To check the remaining power, simply press the side button to reveal the Controls Centre.

Open applications on your smartwatch

Your smartwatch comes with different applications that can help you keep track of your health, workout, etc. To launch any application, simply press the Digital Crown, and then touch the application. Press the Digital Crown once more to return to your Watch's Home Screen. You can also download applications from the Apps Store on your smartwatch.

From the watch face, press to see the Home Screen.

Tap to open an app.

Wake your watch display

You can wake your watch display in the following ways:

❖ Raise your hand. Your smartwatch will go back to sleep when you put your wrist down.
❖ Tap the screen or press the Digital Crown.
❖ Rotate the Digital Crown.

If you do not want your device to wake up when you raise your hand or rotate the Digital Crown, head over to the Settings app ⚙ on your smartwatch, touch Display & Brightness, and then disable Wake on Crown Rotation & Wake on Wrist Raise.

Low Power Mode

Activate Low Power Mode to save battery life. Doing so turns off the Always On feature, background blood oxygen & heart rate measurements, and heart rate alerts. Cellular is turned off till when it's needed - for instance, when you send a message.

Note: The low power mode will turn off automatically when the battery is 80 percent full.

- ❖ Press your watch's side button to reveal the Controls Center.
- ❖ Touch the battery percentage, and then enable Low Power Mode.
- ❖ To confirm your selection, Scroll down, and touch Turn On.
  You can select any of the options to choose how long you want Low Power Mode to be active.

To go back to normal mode simply open the Controls Center, touch the battery percentage, and then deactivate Low Power Mode.

See the time since the last charge

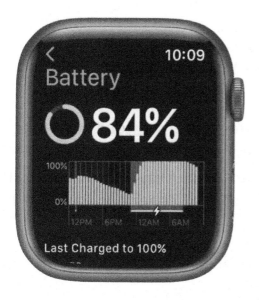

❖ Enter the Settings application on your smartwatch.
❖ Touch Battery.

The battery screen displays the remaining battery percentage, recent battery charge history, and the last time your watch was charged.

Check battery health

❖ Enter the Settings application.

❖ Touch Battery, and then click on Battery Health.

Optimize battery charging

To reduce the battery's aging; your smartwatch makes use of in-device machine learning to learn your charging pattern, with this info it will make sure the battery does not charge above 80% till when you need to use it.

❖ Enter the Settings application on our smartwatch.
❖ Touch Battery, and then touch Battery Health
❖ Activate Optimized Battery Charging.

Stop applications from refreshing in the background

Refreshing applications in the background can use power. You can disable this feature to increase battery life.

❖ Enter the Settings application on our smartwatch.

- ❖ Head over to General, and then touch Background Apps Refresh
- ❖ Deactivate the **Background Apps Refresh** feature to stop all applications on your device from refreshing. Or you can scroll down, and then disable refresh for each application.

Always On

The Always On feature allows your watch to show the watch face, even when you put your wrist down. When you raise your wrist, your smartwatch will start functioning fully.

❖ Enter the Settings application.
❖ Touch Display and Brightness, and then touch the **Always On** button.
❖ Activate the **Always On** feature, and then touch the options below to set them up:
  ➢ Show Apps: Select the applications that should appear when you put your wrist down
  ➢ Show Complications Data.
  ➢ Show Notifications.

Go back to the clock face

Choose how long your smartwatch stays before returning to the clock face from an open application.

❖ Enter the Settings application.
❖ Head over to General> Return to Clock, then scroll down and select any of the options.
❖ You can also press the Digital Crown to go back to the clock face.

By default, the settings you choose will apply to all applications, but you can choose specific times for each application. To do this, touch one of the applications on this screen, touch Custom, and select a setting.

Wake up to your last activity

For some applications, you can programme your smartwatch to go back to where you were in the application before it went to sleep.

❖ Enter the Settings application.
❖ Head over to General> Return to Clock, scroll down and touch one of the applications, then activate **Return to App**

To go back to the clock face, simply stop what you are doing in the application—for instance, cancel a timer, or stop a podcast.

Or, enter the Watch application on your iPhone, touch the **My Watch** tab, and then head over to General> Return to Clock.

Make your watch display on longer

❖ Enter the Settings application.

❖ Touch Display and Brightness, touch Wake Duration, and then select any of the options.

Lock or unlock your smartwatch

Unlock your smartwatch

You can unlock your smartwatch by entering a passcode, or you can programme it to unlock automatically when you unlock your iPhone.

❖ Insert the passcode: Wake your smartwatch, and then type your watch's passcode.
❖ Unlock your smartwatch when you unlock your iPhone: Enter the Watch application on your phone, touch the **My Watch** tab, touch Passcode, and then activate Unlock with iPhone.
Make sure Bluetooth is enabled on both devices and your phone should be within standard Bluetooth range (about 33ft) of your smartwatch to unlock it.

Change your passcode

Follow these steps to change your watch passcode:

❖ Enter the Settings application.
❖ Touch Passcode, touch Change Passcode, and adhere to the directives on your display.

Or, enter the Watch application on your phone, touch the **My Watch** tab, touch Passcode, then touch the **Change Passcode** button and adhere to the directives on your display.

Tip: To use a longer passcode, enter the Settings application on your smartwatch, touch Passcode, and then deactivate **Simple Passcode**.

Turn off the passcode

- ❖ Enter the Settings application.
- ❖ Touch the **Passcode** button, and then touch Turn Off Passcode.

Or, enter the Watch application on your phone, touch the **My Watch** tab, touch Passcode, and then touch Turn Off Passcode.

Auto lock

By default, your smartwatch automatically locks when you are not putting it on. Adhere to the directives below to change the setting.

- ❖ Enter the Settings application.
- ❖ Touch Passcode, and then activate or deactivate the **Wrist Detection** feature

Disabling the wrist detection feature will affect these features:

- When making use of Apple Pay on your smartwatch, you will be asked to insert your passcode when you double-click the side button to authenticate payment.
- Some Activity metrics are not available.

- Heart rate monitoring & notifications are disabled.
- Your smartwatch will no longer lock & unlock automatically.
- Your smartwatch will not automatically make an emergency call even after detecting a hard-impact fall.

Lock it manually

❖ Press your watch's side button to reveal the Controls Centre

❖ Touch the Lock button

Note: To manually lock your smartwatch, you must deactivate Wrist Detection. (Enter the Settings application, touch Passcode, and then disable the Wrist Detection feature.)

You will need to insert your passcode when next you try to use your smartwatch.

You can also lock the screen to prevent accidental taps when exercising. While making use of the Workout application on your smartwatch, simply swipe right, and then touch the **Lock** button. When you begin a swimming exercise, your smartwatch will automatically lock your watch screen with the **Water Lock** feature.

If you forgot your password

If you forget your smartwatch password, you must erase it. Carry out any of the below to erase it:

* Unpair your smartwatch from your phone to delete your watch's password & settings, and then pair it again
* Reset your smartwatch & pair it with your phone.

How to reset your smartwatch if you've forgotten your passcode

❖ Place the smartwatch on the charger & keep it there while you follow these steps.
❖ Long-press the side button till you see the sliders.
❖ Long-press the Digital Crown till **Erase all content & settings** appears.
❖ Touch the **Reset** button, and then touch **Reset** once more to confirm.
❖ Wait for the process to complete, then setup your smartwatch again. When prompted, restore from backup.

How to reset your smartwatch using your paired iPhone

❖ Make sure your iPhone is close to your smartwatch while you follow these steps.
❖ Launch the watch application on your phone, and then touch the **My Watch** button.
❖ Touch General, swipe down, and then touch the **Reset** button.
❖ Touch the **Erase Apple Watch Content & Setting** button, and then touch it once more

in the lower part of your display to confirm. You may need to insert your Apple ID password.

❖ For GPS+ cellular Apple Watch models, choose to keep or turn off the cellular plan:
  ➢ If you do not want to pair your iPhone & smartwatch again, cancel your plan. You may need to call your carrier to cancel your subscription.
  ➢ If you want to sync your smartwatch & phone again, keep your plan.

❖ Wait for the process to complete, then setup your smartwatch again. When prompted, restore from backup.

Erase your data after ten consecutive wrong passcode entries

To protect your data if your smartwatch is stolen or lost, you can set it to delete all data after ten consecutive wrong passcode entries.

❖ Enter the Settings application on your smartwatch.
❖ Touch Passcode, and then activate **Erase Data**.

Change language or region

If you have setup your iPhone to use multiple languages, you can choose the language displayed on your smartwatch.

❖ Enter the Watch application on your phone.
❖ Touch the **My Watch** tab, head over to General> Languages & Region, click on Custom, and then choose one of the languages.

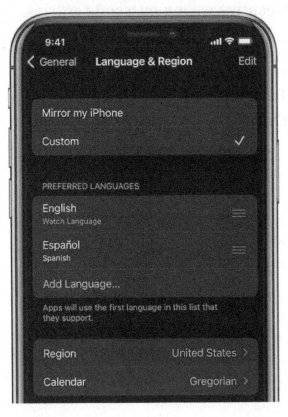

Change Digital Crown or wrists orientation

If you want to wear your smartwatch on your other wrist or you prefer the Digital Crown on the other side, change the settings so that your watch features can function the way it's supposed to.

❖ Enter the Settings application
❖ Head over to General> Orientation.

Or, enter the Watch application on your smartphone, touch the **My Watch** tab, and then head over to General> Watch Orientation.

Wear your Apple Watch

The back of your smartwatch has to touch your skin for features such as electrical and optical heart sensors, Taptic Engine, and Wrist Detection to function properly. Wearing your smartwatch properly— not too loose, not too tight, and with space for your skin to breathe—keeps you comfortable and allows the sensors to function properly.

You may want to tighten your smartwatch when you're exercising, and loosen it a bit when you are done. In addition, the sensors only work when you're wearing your smartwatch on the top of your wrist.

Too loose

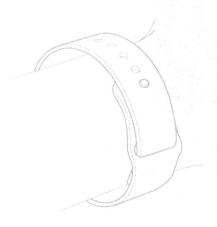

If your smartwatch does not stay in place, or the sensor can't read your heart rate, tighten the band a little.

Perfect

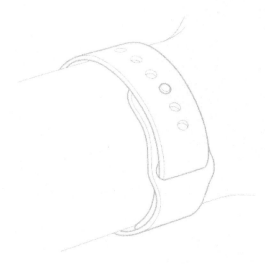

The smartwatch should be snug but comfortable.

Take a screenshot of your smartwatch

❖ Head over to the Settings application on your smartwatch, click on General, click Screenshots, and then activate **Enable Screenshots**.

❖ To take a screenshot, press the Digital Crown and the side button simultaneously.

Screenshots are stored in the Photos application on your phone.

Check for & install software updates

❖ Enter the Watch application on your phone.
❖ Click on **My Watch** tab, head over to General> Software Updates, and if there's an update, click on Download & Install.

Or, enter the Settings application on your smartwatch, then head over to General> Software Updates.

CHANGE YOUR APPLE WATCH BAND

The first thing is to ensure that you are using a band that matches the size of your smartwatch case.

❖ Put your smartwatch face down on a clean surface.
❖ If you have a Link Bracelet, press the release button on the link to split the band in two.
❖ Press and hold the band's release button, and then slide the band across to detach it from your smartwatch.

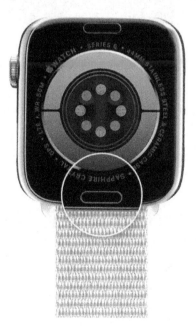

❖ If your watch's band does not slide-out, press the release button once more and make sure you're holding down the button while detaching the band.

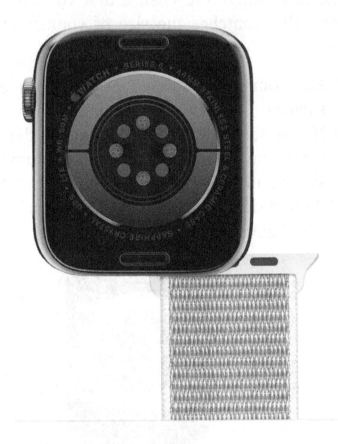

❖ Ensure the band's text is facing you, and then slide the new band in, don't stop till you hear & feel a click.

Solo Loop or braided Solo Loop

If you're using a Solo Loop or a braided Solo Loop, just pull it from the bottom of the band to extend it over your wrist when putting it on & taking it off

Milanese Loop

To completely open the Milanese Loop band, just slide the magnetic closure through the lug or band connector

Removing a link bracelet

You have to separate the Link Bracelet into 2 parts before you remove it from your smartwatch. Try not to twist or force the band while removing it. Follow the directions below to avoid damaging the band.

Close the butterfly closure

To close the butterfly closure, fold it in one side at a time till you hear & feel a click.

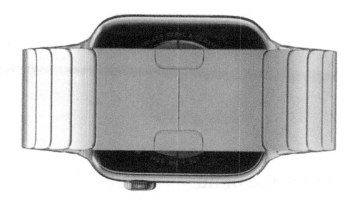

Press and hold the quick-release button

You'll find the quick-release buttons inside the bracelet. You only need to long-press one.

Gently drag the links apart

Press and hold the quick-release button while pulling. Before you remove the band from your smartwatch, first make sure you've separated the band into 2 parts.

Remove the band

Press and hold the band release button, and then slide the band out to detach it.

CUSTOMIZE YOUR SMARTWATCH

Open applications

You can launch any application on your watch from the Home Screen.

From the watch face, press to see the Home Screen.

Tap to open an app.

The Apps Switcher provides fast access to the applications you have used recently.

Show applications in a list or grid view

The Home Screen can show applications in a list or grid view. Adhere to the directives below to pick one:

❖ Press the Digital Crown to enter the Home Screen from your watch face
❖ Rotate the Digital Crown to scroll down to the end of the Home Screen, and then touch List View or Grid View.

Or, enter the Settings application, touch App View, and then select List View or Grid View

Open applications from the Home Screen

❖ Grid View: From the watch face, press the Digital Crown to enter the Home Screen, and then touch the application icon to open the application. If you are already looking at the Home Screen, you can rotate the Digital Crown to see more applications.

From the watch face, press to see the Home Screen.

Tap to open an app.

❖ List view: From the watch face, press the Digital Crown to enter the Home Screen, rotate the Digital Crown, and then touch one of the applications to open it.

Turn the Digital Crown to browse the apps.

Tap to open an app.

Press the Digital Crown to go back to the Home screen from an application, and then press it one more time to go to the watch face.

Launch an application from the App Switcher

❖ Press the Digital Crown twice, then rotate the Digital Crown to scroll through applications in the Apps Switcher.
❖ Touch one of the applications to launch it.

Turn the Digital Crown to see more apps. Tap one to open it.

Remove an application from the Apps Switcher

Press the Digital Crown twice, and then rotate the Digital Crown to the application you plan on removing. Swipe left on the application, and then touch **X**

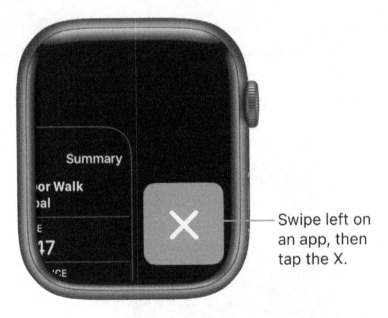

Swipe left on an app, then tap the X.

Organize applications on your smartwatch

Rearrange your applications in grid view

❖ Press the Digital Crown on your smartwatch to go to the Home Screen.

If the screen is in list view, rotate the digital crown to scroll to the end of the Home Screen, and then touch **Grid View**. Or, enter the Settings application on your smartwatch, touch App View, and then touch Grid View.

❖ Long-press an application and then drag the application to another location on the screen.

❖ Press the Digital Crown when you are done.

Touch and hold an app, then drag to a new location.

Or, enter the Watch application on your phone, touch the **My Watch** tab, touch App View, and then touch **Arrangement**. Long-press an application icon, and then drag the application to another location on your screen.

Touch and hold an app, then drag to a new location.

Note: In the List view, applications are arranged alphabetically.

Remove an application from your smartwatch

Long-press the Home Screen, and then touch the **X** to remove the application from your smartwatch. It will remain on your paired iPhone, unless you remove it there as well.

In list view, simply swipe left on an application, and then touch the Trash icon 🗑 to remove the application from your smartwatch.

If you delete an application from your phone, that application is also removed from your smartwatch.

Note: Not all applications can be uninstalled from your smartwatch.

Adjust application settings

❖ Enter the Watch application on your phone.
❖ Touch the **My Watch** tab, and then scroll down to view the applications you've installed.
❖ Touch an application to adjust its settings.

View storage used by the application

You can see how the storage space on your smartwatch is being used—the total usage, the amount remaining, and the amount of storage used by each application.

❖ Enter the Settings application on your smartwatch.
❖ Head over to General> Storage.

Or, enter the Watch application on your phone, touch the **My Watch** tab, then head over to General> Storage.

Get more applications on your smartwatch

You can install applications from the Apps Store on your smartwatch or install applications you already have on your iPhone.

Note: To automatically download the companion iOS version of an application you have added to your smartwatch, enter the Settings application on your smartwatch, touch Apps Store, and then activate Automatic Downloads. Make sure you also have **Automatic Updates** activated to get the latest version of your Apple Watch applications.

Get applications from the Apps Store on your smartwatch

❖ Enter the Apps Store application on your smartwatch.
❖ Rotate the Digital Crown to view featured applications.
❖ Touch one of the collections to see more applications.

❖ Click on the **Get** button to get a free application. Click on the price to buy the application.

If you see a Re-download icon  instead of a price, it means you have already bought the application and can download it again for free.

To look for a specific application, touch the Search button at the upper part of your display, then type, or use the Dictation or Scribble feature to type the name of the application. You can also click on a category to view subcategories of applications.

To use the Scribble feature, swipe up from the lower edge of your display, and then touch the **Scribble** button.

Install applications already on your iPhone

By default, applications on your phone that have a WatchOS application available are installed automatically and appear on your watch's Home Screen. To instead choose to install certain applications, simply adhere to the directives below:

❖ Enter the Watch application on your phone.
❖ Touch the **My Watch** tab, touch the **General** button, and then deactivate Automatic App Install.
❖ Touch the **My Watch** tab, and then scroll down to the **Available Apps** section.
❖ Click on the **Install** button beside the applications you would like to install.

Tell the time on your watch

There are many ways to tell the time on your smartwatch.

❖ Raise your hand: The time will appear on your watch face and in the upper-right corner of many applications.

❖ Hear the time: Enter the Settings application on your smartwatch, touch Clock, and then activate the **Speak Time** feature. Hold 2 of your fingers on the watch face to hear the time.

You can set your smartwatch to play chimes on the hour. To do this, simply enter the Settings application on your smartwatch, touch Clock, and then activate the **Chimes** feature. Touch Sounds to pick one of the options.

❖ Feel the time: To feel the time tapped on your wrist when you turn on silent mode on your smartwatch, simply enter the Settings application, touch the **Clock** button, touch the **Taptic Time** button, activate Taptic Time, and then select one of the options.

Note: If Taptic-Time is turned off, your smartwatch might be set to always say the time. To enable Taptic Time, first enter the Settings application, touch Clock, and then activate **Controls with Silent Mode** below Speak Time.

❖ Use Siri: Raise your hand & say "What's the time?"

View the time in other cities

You can use the World Clock application to check the time in cities around the world

❖ Enter the World Clock application.

❖ Touch the List icon , and then rotate the Digital Crown to scroll.

❖ Touch one of the cities in the list to find more info about the city, including sunrise & sunset time.

❖ When you are done, touch the < button in the upper left corner or swipe to the right to go back to the list of cities.

Change the city abbreviation

Adhere to the directives below to change the city abbreviation used on your smartwatch:

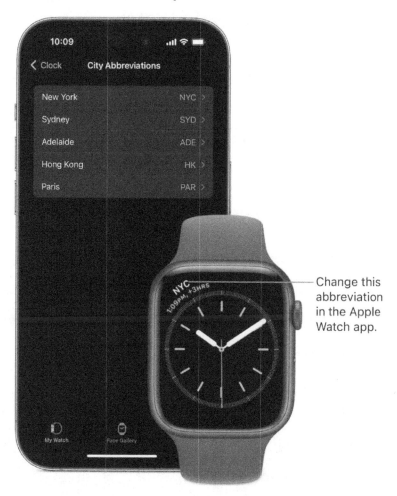

Change this abbreviation in the Apple Watch app.

* ❖ Enter the Watch application on your phone.
* ❖ Touch the **My Watch** tab, then head over to Clock> City Abbreviations.

❖ Touch any of the cities to change its abbreviation.

Stopwatch on Apple Watch

Your smartwatch can time full activity (up to 11 hours), track laps or split times, and then display the results as a graph, a list, or directly on your watch face.

Open and select a stopwatch

❖ Enter the Stopwatch application on your smartwatch.
❖ Rotate the Digital Crown to select another format
   You can pick Digital, Hybrid, or Analog.

Start, stop & restart the stopwatch

Enter the Stopwatch application, rotate the Digital Crown to select one of the formats, and then carry out any of the below:

❖ Start: Touch the **Start** icon ▶ .

❖ Record Laps: Touch the **Lap** icon ● .

❖ Record the final time: Touch the Stop icon ■ .

❖ Reset the stopwatch: When the stopwatch stops, touch the Reset icon ↺ .

The timing will continue even if you return to the watch face or open another application.

Start or stop the stopwatch.

Record lap times.

Set Timers

You can use the Timers application to keep track of time.

Quickly set a timer

❖ Enter the Timers application.
❖ To start the timer quickly, touch one of the durations or touch a timer you have recently used under Recent. To create a custom timer, scroll down and click the **Add** button .

When a timer goes off, you can touch the "Repeat Timer" button⟳ to start the timer for the same duration.

Pause or end a timer

❖ When the timer starts, enter the Timers application.

❖ Touch the "Pause" icon ‖ to pause, click on the "Play" icon ▶ to continue, or the "Done" icon ✕ to end.

Create a custom timer

❖ Enter the Timers application.

❖ Touch the **Add** button ⊕

❖ Touch seconds, minutes, or hours; rotate the Digital Crown to adjust.

❖ Touch the Start button.

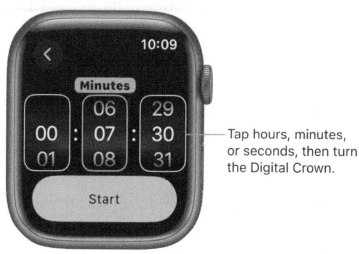

Tap hours, minutes, or seconds, then turn the Digital Crown.

Create multiple timers

❖ Enter the Timers application.
❖ Create & begin a timer.
Tip: To give the timer a name like Barbeque, use Siri to create the timer. Raise your smartwatch and say "Set a 13-minute [Name of Timer] timer."
❖ Touch the Add button⊕ to go back to the Timer screen, and then create & start another timer.

Touch the Back icon ◉ to show all your running timers on the Timers display. Click on the "Pause" icon ‖ to pause the timer and click on the "Play" icon ► to resume.

To remove a timer that appears on your Timers display, swipe to the left, and then touch the **X** button.

Set Alarm

- ❖ Enter the Alarms application.
- ❖ Click on the **Add Alarm** button ⊕.
- ❖ Touch PM or AM, and then touch the minutes or hours.
  This step isn't necessary when making use of a 24-hour time.
- ❖ Rotate the Digital Crown to adjust, and then touch the Check button ✓.

❖ To activate or deactivate the alarm, touch its switch. Or touch the alarm time to set snooze, label, & repeat options.

Turn off snooze

When an alarm starts playing, you can touch the **Snooze** button to wait a few minutes before the alarm starts playing again. If you do not want to allow snooze, adhere to the directives below:

❖ Enter the Alarms application.
❖ Touch the alarm in the alarms list, and then disable Snooze.

Delete an alarm

❖ Enter the Alarms application.
❖ Touch the alarm in the alarms list.
❖ Scroll down, and then touch the **Delete** button.

Skip a wake-up alarm

If you set a wake-up alarm that is part of your sleep routine, you can skip the alarm for a day.

❖ Enter the Alarms application.
❖ Touch the alarm under Alarms, then touch the **Skip for Tonight** button.

See the same alarms on your iPhone & smartwatch

❖ Set the alarm on your smartphone.
❖ Enter the Watch application on your smartphone
❖ Touch the **My Watch** tab, touch the **Clock** button, and then activate the **Push Alerts from iPhone** feature.

Your smartwatch will alert you when the alarm goes off so you can dismiss or snooze the alarm.

Turn your smartwatch into a nightstand watch with alarm

❖ Enter the Settings application on your smartwatch.
❖ Head over to General> Nightstand Mode, and then activate Nightstand mode.

When your smartwatch is connected to its charger while nightstand mode is activated, it'll display the charging status, current date & time, and the alarm time you've set. Touch the screen or lightly nudge your smartwatch to see the time.

If you set an alarm, your smartwatch in Nightstand Mode will gently wake you up with a unique sound. When you hear the sound, press the side button to turn off the alarm, or press the Digital Crown for Snooze to give yourself some time to rest.

Press to snooze.

Press to turn off alarm.

Control Center

Controls Center provides a simple way to check your watch battery level, select a Focus, turn on the flashlight, silence your smartwatch, etc.

Apple Watch   Apple Watch with Cellular

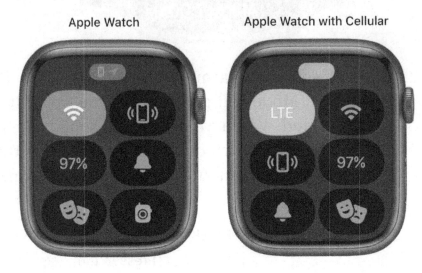

Open & close the Controls Center

❖ Enter Controls Centre: Press your watch's side button.
❖ Close Controls Centre: Swipe down from the upper part of your display, or press the Digital Crown.

Check the Controls Centre status

The icons in the upper part of the Controls Centre provide info about the common configuration status of your smartwatch. For instance, a small group of icons can indicate that your smartwatch is connected to your iPhone or Airplane Mode is activated.

To get info, simply touch the icons in the Controls Centre.

Rearrange Control Center

You can reorder the icons in the Controls Centre by adhering to the directives below:

❖ Press your watch's side button to reveal the Controls Center.

❖ Scroll down, and then touch the **Edit** button.

❖ Long-press one of the buttons, and then drag the button to another location.

❖ Touch the **Done** button when you are done.

Remove the Control Center buttons

Adhere to the directives below to remove the buttons in the Controls Centre:

❖ Press your watch's side button to reveal the Controls Center.

❖ Scroll down, and then touch the **Edit** button

❖ Touch the Erase icon  in the edge of the button you want to erase.

❖ Touch the **Done** button when you are done.

To restore a deleted button, open the Controls Centre, click on the **Edit** button, and then click on the Add icon in the corner of the button you would like to restore. When you are done, touch the **Done** button.

Activate Airplane mode

Some airlines will allow you to travel with your smartwatch switched on if it's in airplane mode. By default, activating Airplane mode disables WiFi & cellular and keeps Bluetooth enabled. However, you can change what settings are activated & deactivated when you enable airplane mode.

❖ Activate Airplane mode: Press your watch's side button to reveal the Controls Center, and then touch the Airplane Mode button ✈

Turn Airplane Mode on or off.

❖ Put both your smartwatch & phone in Airplane Mode in one step: Enter the Watch application on your phone, touch the **My Watch** tab, head over to General, touch Airplane Mode, and then activate the **Mirror iPhone** feature. When both devices are within standard Bluetooth range (around 33ft), any time you activate Airplane Mode on one of them, the other will automatically switch on.

❖ Change which settings are activated or deactivated in Airplane Mode: On your smartwatch, enter the Settings application, touch Airplane Mode, and choose whether to activate or deactivate Bluetooth or Wifi by default when Airplane mode is turned on.

To enable or disable Bluetooth or Wifi while your smartwatch is in Airplane mode, enter the Settings application, and then touch Bluetooth or Wifi.

When you activate Airplane mode, the Airplane mode icon ✈ will appear in the upper part of your display.

Note: Even after activating Mirror iPhone, you must deactivate Airplane Mode separately on your phone & smartwatch.

Use the flashlight on your smartwatch

Use your watch's flashlight to illuminate objects close to you.

❖ Switch on the flashlight: Press your watch's side button to reveal the Controls Center, and then touch the Flashlight button 🔦 . Swipe left to select one of the modes.
❖ Rotate the Digital Crown to change the brightness level.
❖ Switch off the flashlight: Press the side button or Digital Crown.

Use theater mode

Theater mode stops your screen from turning on when you raise your hand. It also activates silent mode.

Press your watch's side button to reveal the Controls Center, touch the Theater Mode button , and then touch Theater Mode.

Turn theater mode on or off.

When you activate theater mode, you'll see the theater status icon in the upper part of your display.

To wake your smartwatch when theater mode is enabled, touch the screen, rotate the Digital Crown, or press the side button or Digital Crown.

Disconnected from WiFi

Press your watch's side button to reveal the Controls Center, and then touch the Wifi button 📶 in the Controls Center.

Tap to disconnect from Wi-Fi.

Enable silent mode

Press your watch's side button to reveal the Controls Center, and then touch the Silent Mode button 🔔 in the Controls Center.

Note: If your smartwatch is connected to power, timers & alarms will still sound even when silent mode is turned on.

Or, enter the Watch application on your phone, touch the **My Watch** tab, touch **Sound & Haptic**, and then activate **Silent mode**.

Tip: When you receive a notification, you can quickly silence your device by resting your palm on your smartwatch screen for about 3 seconds. You will feel a tap to confirm that your smartwatch has been silenced. Ensure you activate the **Cover to Mute** feature on your smartwatch—enter the Settings application, touch Sound & Haptic, and then activate Cover to Mute.

Find your iPhone

The **Precision Finding** feature allows your smartwatch to ping an iPhone 15 that's close by and get directions to the phone.

❖ Press your watch's side button to reveal the Controls Centre, and then touch the Ping iPhone button . Your phone will play a sound and if your smartwatch is within range, its screen will show a heading & distance to your phone—77ft, for instance.

❖ Touch the Ping iPhone button in the lower right edge to ring your phone as you track it.

❖ Follow the directions on your watch screen, and make changes as the heading moves.

When you get close to your phone, your watch's display will turn green and the iPhone will ping twice.

Hint: In a dark place? Long-press the Ping iPhone button  and your iPhone will flash as well.

If your phone is not in range with your smartwatch, try making use of Find My from iCloud.com.

Find your Apple Watch

iOS 17 allows iPhone users to find their Apple Watch if it is close to them.

❖ Enter the Settings application on your phone.
❖ Touch Controls Centre, scroll down, and then touch the Add icon ● beside **Ping My Watch**.
❖ When you want to locate your smartwatch, open the Control Centre on your phone, and then touch the **Ping Apple Watch** button ⟨◌⟩.

Adhere to the directives below to locate your smartwatch with Find My:

❖ Enter the Watch application on your phone
❖ Touch the **My Watch** tab, and then touch the **All Watches** button

❖ Touch the Info icon ⓘ beside your smartwatch, and then touch **Find My Apple Watch.**
❖ In the Find My application on your phone, touch your smartwatch to see where it is on a map.

If the map tells you that your smartwatch is close to you, touch the **Play Sound** button

Focus

The Focus feature can help you to focus when you want to concentrate on a task. Focus can lessen distractions & let other applications & people know that you are busy.

You can select from the available Focus modes or create one on your phone.

Note: If you would like to share your Focus settings with all the Apple devices signed in with your Apple ID, launch the Settings application on your smartphone, click on the **Focus** button, and then enable the **Share Across Devices** feature.

Enable or disable a Focus

❖ Press your watch's side button to reveal the Controls Center.
❖ Long-press the current **Focus** button.
If no focus mode is active, the Controls Centre will show the DND button 🌙.

❖ Touch one of the Focus modes

❖ Select one of the Focus options.

To disable a Focus mode, simply touch the Focus button in the Controls Centre.

When a Focus mode is turned on, its icon will appear in the upper part of the watch face, beside the time in applications, & in the Controls Centre.

Create your own focus

❖ Enter the Settings application on your phone, and then touch the **Focus** button.

❖ Touch the Add icon ┬, select one of the Focus modes, and then adhere to the directives on your display

Select a focus watch face

You can set a watch face to appear when a specific Focus mode is activated. For instance, when you activate Work Focus mode, your smartwatch can show a simple watch face.

- ❖ Launch the Settings application on your iPhone, and then tap on the **Focus** button.
- ❖ Touch one of the Focus modes, and then touch Choose under the Watch image.
- ❖ Select one of the watch faces, and then touch the **Done** button

Create a Focus schedule

You can schedule when a Focus mode activates on your smartwatch. For instance, you can set the Work Focus mode to automatically turn on at 9:30AM & turn off at 12:30PM, from Monday to Friday. From 12:30PM to 1:30PM you may have no Focus. Then, begin the Work Focus mode again from 1:30PM to 4:30PM, Monday-Thursday.

❖ Head over to the Settings application on your smartwatch.

❖ Click on **Focus**, and then touch one of the Focus mode
❖ Tap on the **Add New** button.
❖ Click on the From & To options and insert when you want the Focus mode to automatically activate & deactivate.

❖ Scroll down the list, and select the days you want the Focus to be active.

❖ Tap on the < button in the top left corner of the display to save the options you've set.
❖ Repeat the steps above to add more events to the Focus mode.

Delete or turn off a Focus schedule

❖ Turn off a Focus schedule: On your smartwatch, head over to the Settings application, touch the **Focus** button, and then touch a Focus mode. Touch one of the schedules, scroll down, and then deactivate **Enabled**.

Activate **Enabled** when you want to turn on the schedule again.

❖ Erase a Focus schedule: On your smartwatch, head over to the Settings application, tap on the **Focus** button, and then touch a Focus mode. Touch one of the schedules, scroll down, and then touch the **Delete** button.

Change the brightness level, size of text, haptics, & sounds on your smartwatch

Change brightness & text size

Head over to the Settings application on your smartwatch, and then touch **Display and Brightness** to make adjustments to the following:

- ❖ Brightness: Click on the Brightness control to make adjustments, or touch the slider, and then rotate the Digital Crown.
- ❖ Text size: Touch the **Text Size** option, and then touch the letters or rotate the Digital Crown.
- ❖ Bold Text: Enable the **Bold Text** feature.

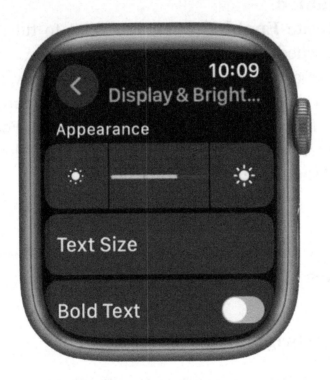

Or, enter the Watch application on your phone, touch the **My Watch** tab, touch Display and Brightness, and then change the text & brightness level.

Adjust the sound

❖ Head over to the Settings application on your smartwatch.
❖ Touch **Sound and Haptics**
❖ Touch the volume control in the **Alert Volume** section or touch the slider, and then rotate the Digital Crown to make the adjustments.

Or, launch the Watch application on your smartphone, touch Sound and Haptics, and then slide the Alert Volume slider.

Change haptic intensity

You can make adjustments to the haptics strength —or wrist taps—your smartwatch uses for alerts & notifications.

❖ Head over to the Settings application on your smartwatch.
❖ Click on **Sounds and Haptic**, and then activate **Haptic Alerts**.
❖ Choose one of the options (Prominent or Default)

Or, launch the Watch application on your smartphone, touch the **My Watch** tab, touch Sound and Haptics, and then select one of the options (Prominent or Default).

Enable or disable Digital Crown haptics

On your smartwatch, you feel clicks when you rotate the Digital Crown to scroll. To disable or enable this feature, simply adhere to the directives below:

❖ Head over to the Settings application on your smartwatch.

❖ Click on **Sounds and Haptic**, and then activate or deactivate **Crown Haptics**.
You can also activate or deactivate systems haptics

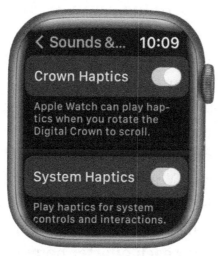

You can also enter the Watch application on your phone, touch the **My Watch** tab, touch Sound & Haptics, and then activate or deactivate Crown Haptics.

Use Taptic Time

When you put your smartwatch in Silent mode, it can tap out the time on your wrist with a set of unique taps.

❖ Head over to the Settings application on your smartwatch.
❖ Touch the **Clock** button, scroll down, and then touch Taptic Time.
❖ Activate the **Taptic Time** feature, and then select one of the settings—Morse Code, Terse, or Digits.
  ➢ Digits: Your smartwatch will long tap your wrist for every ten hours, short tap for every hour that follows, long tap for every ten minutes, and then short tap for every minute that follows.
  ➢ Terse: Your smartwatch will long tap your wrist for every 5 hours, short tap your wrist for the remaining hours, and then long tap you for each quarter hour.
  ➢ Morse code: Your smartwatch will tap each digit of the time on your wrist in Morse code.

To set it up on your iPhone, simply launch the Watch application, touch the **My Watch** tab,

head over to Clock> Taptic Time, and then
activate it.

See & respond to notifications on your smartwatch

Respond to messages when they arrive

❖ If you hear an alert sound, just raise your hand
to check it.
How the alert appears depends on whether
your screen is idle or active.
➢ Active screen: You will see a little banner at
the upper part of your screen.
➢ Idle screen: You will see a full-screen
notification.

❖ Click on the notification to go through it.

❖ Swipe down on a notification to clear it. Or scroll down, and touch the **Dismiss** button at the end of the notification.

View notifications you have not responded to

If you do not respond to a notification the moment you receive it, the notification will be stored in the **Notifications Center**. A red dot at the upper part of your watch face indicates that you have unread notifications. Adhere to the directives below to view them:

Swipe down to view unread notifications.

❖ Swipe down from the watch face to reveal the Notifications Center. From another screen, long-press the top of your display, and then swipe down.

Note: You cannot enter the Notifications Center from your watch's Home screen. Instead, go back to the watch face or launch an application, and then open the Notifications Center.

❖ Swipe down or up or rotate the Digital crown to scroll through the available notifications.

❖ Touch one of the notifications to go through it or reply to the sender.

Tip: Siri can help you read notifications from the Notifications Centre. Simply say "Read my notification".

To delete one of the notifications from the Notifications Centre without reading it, simply swipe the notification to the left, and then touch the **X** button. To delete all the notifications, scroll to the beginning, and then touch the **Clear All** button.

Tip: To prevent the red dot from popping up on the watch face, enter the Settings application on your smartwatch, touch the **Notifications** button, and then disable **Notifications Indicator**.

Swipe down to view unread notifications.

Mute all notifications on your smartwatch

Press your watch's side button to reveal the Controls Center, and then touch the Ring button

Your watch will still tap your wrist when it receives a notification. Adhere to the directives below to prevent sound & taps:

❖ Press your watch's side button to reveal the Controls Center

❖ Touch the DND button ☾ or the active Focus mode

❖ Touch Do Not Disturb, and then select one of the options — On for an hour, On until I leave, etc.

Tip: When a notification arrives, you can quickly silence your smartwatch by placing your palm on the watch's screen for about 3 seconds. You'll feel a tap to confirm that your device has been silenced. Ensure you've activated the **Cover to Mute** feature—head over to the Settings application on your smartwatch, touch Sound and Haptics, and then activate the **Cover to Mute** feature.

Display notifications on your watch's lock screen

You can choose how notifications appear on your watch's lock screen.

❖ Head over to the Settings application on your smartwatch.
❖ Touch the **Notifications** button
❖ Select the options below:
  ➤ Show summary when locked.
  ➤ Touch to Show Full Notifications: When you lift your wrist to view an alert, you'll see a summary, followed by full details after a few seconds. For instance, when you receive a notification, you'll see who sent the message

first, and then the message will appear. Activate this option to prevent the full message from appearing unless you touch it.

➢ Show Notifications on your Wrist Down.

Use Smart Stack to display relevant widgets on your smartwatch

Smart Stack is a group of widgets that makes use of info like the time, place, and your task to automatically show widgets that are relevant for that time in your day. For instance, in the morning the, Weather will display the forecast, or when you travel, Smart Stack will display the boarding pass from your wallet.

Open Smart Stack

❖ Press your watch's Digital Crown to display the watch face.
❖ Rotate the Digital Crown till you see widgets
❖ Scroll till you see the widget you want, and then touch it to open its application.

Add & remove widgets

Scroll down from the watch face, long-press the Smart Stack, and then carry out any of the below:

❖ Add widgets: Touch the Add icon +, and then touch one of the featured widgets or touch any of the applications under All Apps.
❖ Remove Widget: Click on the Remove button ⊖.

Touch the **Done** button when you are done.

Manage your Apple ID settings

You can check out & change the info associated with your Apple ID.

Change contact info

❖ Enter the Settings application on your smartwatch.
❖ Touch [your name], touch Personal Information, and then carry out any of the below:
  ➢ Make changes to your name: Touch your name, and then touch Last, Middle, or First.
  ➢ Change your date of birth: Touch Birthday, and then insert another date.
  ➢ Receive notifications, offers, or the Apple News newsletter: Touch Communication Preferences. You can activate Announcements; recommendations for TV, songs, applications, etc.; or subscribe to the Apple News Newsletter.

Manage your Apple ID password & security

❖ Enter the Settings application on your smartwatch.
❖ Touch **[your name]**.
❖ Touch **Sign In and Security**
  The e-mail addresses & numbers linked to your Apple ID will be displayed, with their status

❖ Carry out any of the below:
  ➢ Remove one of the e-mail addresses: touch the e-mail address, then touch the **Remove Email Address** button.
  ➢ Add a phone number or e-mail address: Touch Add Emails or Phone Number, choose to add a number or e-mail address, touch **Next**, insert the details, and then touch Done.
  ➢ Make changes to your Apple ID passcode: Touch the **Change Password** button, and then adhere to the directives on your display.
  ➢ Hide your e-mail address: Click on **Forward To**, and then select one of the addresses.
  ➢ Change "**Sign in with Apple**" settings for a site or application: Touch the **Sign in with Apple** button, and then select one of the applications. Touch the **Stop Using Apple ID** button to remove your Apple ID from the application.
  ➢ Touch Two-Factor Authentication, and then touch the **Get Verification Code** button to receive a verification code to log in on iCloud.com or another device.

➤ Add or edit a trusted number: Touch 2-Factor Authentication, touch the trusted phone number, authenticate when asked to, and then touch the **Remove Phone Number** button. To add another trusted number, touch the **Add a Trusted Phone Number** button.

View & manage subscriptions

❖ Enter the Settings application on your smartwatch.
❖ Touch [your name].
❖ Touch the **Subscriptions** button, and then scroll down to view your subscriptions
❖ Touch one of the subscriptions to get more info about it, like its cost & length, and make changes to its options.
❖ Click on the **Cancel Subscriptions** button to end your subscription.

View & manage your devices

❖ Enter the Settings application on your smartwatch.
❖ Touch [your name].

❖ Scroll down, and then touch one of the devices to show info about it.
❖ Touch the **Remove from Account** button if you see a device that you do not recognize.

Handwashing feature

Your smartwatch can detect when you start washing your hands and advise you to continue for twenty seconds, which is the recommended time by the World Health Organization. Your smartwatch can also alert you if you have not washed your hands within minutes of getting home.

Activate the Hand-washing feature

❖ Enter the Settings application.

❖ Touch the **Handwashing** button, and then enable the **Handwashing Timer** feature.

When your smartwatch notices that you have started washing your hands, it will start a twenty-second timer. If you stop washing your hands in less than twenty seconds, you are advised to complete the task.

Receive hand-washing alerts

Your smartwatch can remind you to wash your hands when you get home.

❖ Enter the Settings application.

❖ Click on the **Handwashing** button, and then activate the **Handwashing Reminders** feature.

Note: To get hand-washing reminders, please add your address to your **My Card** in the **Contact** application on your iPhone.

To view a report of your average hand-washing time, simply enter the Health application on your phone, head over to Browse> Other Data, and then touch the **Handwashing** button.

Connect to WiFi

Connecting your smartwatch to Wifi, allows you to use many of its features even when you're not with your iPhone.

Select a WiFi network

❖ Press your watch's side button to reveal the Controls Centre

❖ Press & hold the WiFi button 🛜 , and then touch one of the available WiFi networks.

❖ If a password is needed before you can connect, simply carry out any of the below:
  ➢ Use the keyboard on your smartwatch to insert the passcode.
  ➢ Click on the Password button 📍, and then select one of the passwords from the list.
  ➢ Use your iPhone's keyboard to insert the passcode.
❖ Touch the **Join** button.

Forget a network

❖ Press your watch's side button to reveal the Controls Centre
❖ Press & hold the WiFi button 📶, and then touch the name of the network you've connected to.
❖ Touch the **Forget This Network** button.

Pair your smartwatch with Bluetooth speakers or headphones

Play audio from your smartwatch on a Bluetooth speaker or headphone.

Connect a Bluetooth headphone or speaker

Adhere to the directives that came with the speaker or headphone to put the device in discovery mode. Once your Bluetooth device is ready, follow the directives below:

❖ Enter the Settings application, and then touch Bluetooth.
❖ Touch the name of the device in the list when it appears.

Or, touch the AirPlay button 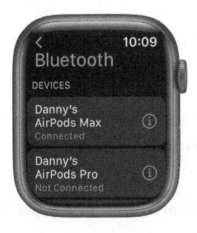 on the Play screens of the Podcasts, Now Playing, Music, & Audiobooks application to enter the Bluetooth settings.

Select an output sound

❖ Press your watch's side button to reveal the Controls Centre

❖ Touch the Airplay button, and then select the device you would like to use.

Controls the volume of your headphone

❖ Press your watch's side button to reveal the Controls Centre

❖ Tap on the Headphone Volume button while listening to your headphones
A meter will display the current volume of your headphone.

Reduce loud sounds

Your smartwatch can limit your headphone audio loudness to a certain decibel level.

❖ Navigate to the Settings application on your smartwatch.
❖ Head over to Sound & Haptic> Headphones Safety, and then touch the **Reduce Loud Sounds** button.

❖ Activate the **Reduce Loud Sounds** feature, and then select a level.

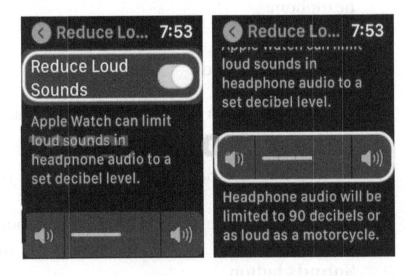

Check for loud headphone notifications

If your headphones are too loud, your smartwatch will send you a headphone alert and automatically lower the volume to protect your ears.

Adhere to the directives below to see info about headphone notifications:

❖ Enter the Settings application on your smartwatch
❖ Head over to Sound & Haptic> Headphones Safety, then touch Last Six Months in the **Headphone Notifications** section.

Or, enter the Health application on your phone, touch the **Browse** button, touch the **Hearing** button, click on Headphone Notifications, and then touch one of the notifications.

Handoff task from your smartwatch

The **Handoff** feature allows you to switch from one Apple device to another without losing focus on what you are doing. For instance, you can start replying to an e-mail in the Mail application on your smartwatch and finish replying to the email on your iPhone. Follow these directives to use the Handoff feature.

❖ Unlock your iPhone.
❖ Swipe up from the lower edge of your screen & stop to display the Apps Switcher (For Face ID iPhone).

Or, double-click the Home button to display the Apps Switcher (For Home-button iPhone)
❖ Click on the button in the lower part of your display to launch the same item on your phone.

Tip: If you can't find the button in the Apps Switcher, ensure you activate the **Handoff** feature for your iPhone in the Settings application> General> AirPlay and Handoff.

Handoff is enabled by default. To deactivate Handoff, enter the Watch application on your phone, touch the **My Watch** tab, touch the **General** button, and then deactivate **Enable Handoff**.

Unlock your MacOS device with your smartwatch

If you own a Mac running MacOS 10.130 or after, you can use your smartwatch to unlock it when it wakes from sleep. You must make sure you're signed in to iCloud with the same Apple ID on both devices.

Activate the Auto Unlock feature

❖ Make sure of the following:
  ➢ Make sure you activate Bluetooth & WiFi on your MacOS device.

➢ Make sure you're signed in to iCloud with the same Apple ID on both devices, and your Apple ID uses 2-factor authentication.

➢ Make sure your smartwatch uses a passcode.

❖ Carry out any of the below:

➢ If your device is making use of MacOS 13.0 or after, select Apple menu> Systems Setting, and then click on **Login Password**.

➢ If your device is making use of MacOS 12.0 or before, select Apple menu> Systems Preference, click on Security & Privacy, and then click on General.

❖ Select the **Use Apple Watch to unlock applications & your Mac** option.

If you own multiple Apple Watches, choose the watches you would like to use to unlock your applications & MacOS device.

If your Apple ID does not have 2-factor authentication, simply adhere to the directives on your display, and then select the checkbox once more.

Unlock your MacOS device

While putting on your smartwatch, simply wakeup your MacOS device—you don't have to type your password.

Tip: Ensure your smartwatch is unlocked & on your wrist and you are close to your MacOS device.

Unlock your iPhone with Apple Watch

To let your smartwatch unlock your phone when an obstruction is stopping Face ID from recognizing your face, do the below:

❖ On your iPhone, head over to the Settings application, tap on Face ID & Passcode, and then insert your passcode.
❖ Scroll down to the **Unlock with Apple Watch** segment, and then enable the setting for your smartwatch.

If you have multiple watches, simply activate the setting for each of them.
❖ To unlock your phone, ensure you are putting on your smartwatch, wake your phone, and then stare at your phone's display.

Your smartwatch will tap your wrist to inform you that your phone has been unlocked.

Note: To unlock your phone, your smartwatch needs to have a password, be on your wrist & unlocked, and be near your phone.

Use your watch with a cellular network

With a **GPS + Cellular** Apple Watch & a mobile connection to the carrier used by your phone, you can stream podcasts & songs, use Walkie-Talkie, reply to messages, make calls, & more on your smartwatch even without a WiFi connection or your phone.

Add your smartwatch to your cellular plan

Follow the directions below to activate cellular service:

❖ Enter the Watch application on your smartphone.
❖ Click on the **My Watch** tab, and then touch **Cellular**.

Adhere to the directives to get more info about your carrier's service plan and turn on cellular for your smartwatch.

Activate or deactivate cellular

❖ Press your watch's side button to reveal the Controls Centre
❖ Click on the Cellular button ((( ))), and then enable or disable Cellular.

The Cellular button will turn green when your smartwatch is connected to the cellular and your phone is not close by.

The Cellular button turns green when you have a connection. The green dots show the signal strength.

The green dots show the cellular connection's signal strength.

Check your mobile data usage

❖ Navigate to the Settings application on your smartwatch.
❖ Click on **Cellular**, and then scroll down to view how much data you've used so far.

Control your watch with your iPhone

The **Apple Watch Mirroring** feature allows users to control their smartwatch with assistive features like Switch Control & Voice Control, and use inputs like head tracking, sound actions, voice commands, and more as alternatives to tapping the watch's screen.

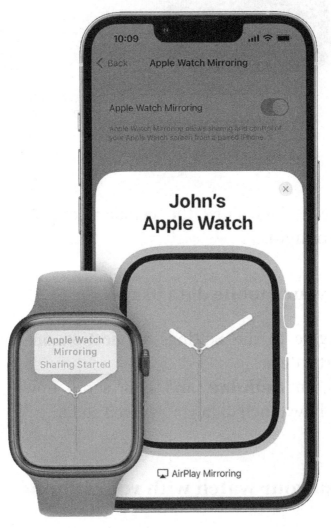

❖ Enter the **Setting** application on your paired iPhone.
❖ Head over to Accessibility> Apple Watch Mirroring, and then activate the **Apple Watch Mirroring** feature.

An image showing your watch's screen will appear on your phone. You can use basic gestures to control your watch from your phone.

❖ Scroll: Swipe down or up on the screen.
❖ Press the Digital Crown: Touch the Digital Crown on the screen.
❖ Swipe between screens: Swipe to the right or left on the screen.
❖ Use Siri: Long-press the Digital Crown on the screen.
❖ Press the side button: Touch the side button on the screen.

Use your smartwatch to control nearby devices

You can use your smartwatch to control your iPad or iPhone.

- ❖ Enter the Settings application on your smartwatch.
- ❖ Head over to Accessibility> Control Nearby devices.

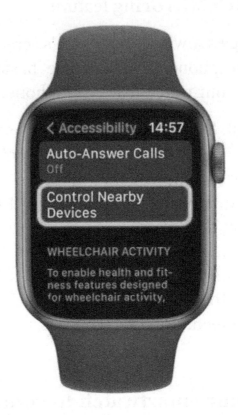

You must make sure you're signed in to iCloud with the same Apple ID on your iPad, iPhone, & watch, and both devices must be on the same network.

- ❖ Select a device if a lot of devices are close by, and then touch a button.

The buttons replicate the controls on your device & include:

- ❖ Home button
- ❖ Apps Switcher
- ❖ Notification Centre
- ❖ Controls Centre
- ❖ Siri
- ❖ Options(like media playback controls & gestures)

AssistiveTouch

With the **AssistiveTouch** feature, you can use your smartwatch if you have trouble pressing the buttons or tapping the display. The sensors inside the smartwatch can help you answer calls, launch an actions menu, & control a pointer on the screen with hand gestures.

With the **AssistiveTouch** feature, you can do these & other actions:

❖ Touch the screen
❖ Swipe through screens
❖ Use Apple Pay
❖ Click & rotate the Digital Crown
❖ Display applications

- ❖ Summon Siri
- ❖ Run Siri shortcuts
- ❖ Gain access to the Controls Centre, Notifications Centre, & the Dock.

Setup AssistiveTouch

- ❖ Enter the Settings application on your smartwatch.
- ❖ Head over to Accessibility

❖ Touch AssistiveTouch, and then activate the **AssistiveTouch** feature.

❖ Touch the **Hand Gestures** button, and then activate the **Hand Gestures** feature.

Tip: To get more info about how to use hand gestures, touch the **Learn More** button under the Hand Gestures toggle, and then touch each gesture. After touching a gesture, an animation will show you how to perform the gesture.

Or

❖ Launch the Apple Watch application on your phone, touch the **My Watch** tab, and head over to Accessibility

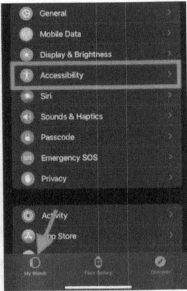

❖ Touch AssistiveTouch, and then activate the **AssistiveTouch** feature.

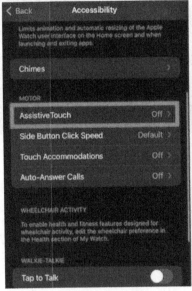

Use AssistiveTouch with your watch

With the **AssistiveTouch** feature & **Hand Gestures** activated, navigate your smartwatch with the default gestures below:

❖ Clench: Tap

❖ Double-clench: Display the Actions Menu
❖ Pinch: Forward.

❖ Double-pinch: Go back

For instance, with the Meridian watch-face showing, use the **AssistiveTouch** feature with the Activity application by adhering to the directives below:

❖ Clench twice to activate the **AssistiveTouch** feature.
   You'll see a highlight around the Music complication.
❖ Pinch thrice to move to the Activity's complication and then clench to touch it.
❖ When your watch opens the Activity application, clench twice to display the Actions Menu.

- Pinch to highlight Systems action, pinch once more to highlight the Scroll Up action, and then clench to choose it.
- Clench once to enter the next screen.
- Pinch twice to display the Actions menu. Pinch or double pinch to surf through the actions
- Select the Press Crown action, and then clench to go back to the watch face.

Use the Motion Pointer

The Motion Pointer allows you to control your smartwatch by tilting your watch down & up and side to side. For instance, you can use the **Motion Pointer** feature to surf through the Stopwatch application by adhering to the directives below:

- With the watch face showing & your smartwatch in list view, clench twice to enable the **AssistiveTouch** feature.
- Clench-twice again to display the Actions menu
- Clench once to choose the Press Crown action and open your watch's Home Screen.

- ❖ Clench twice to display the Actions Menu, keep pinching till you select the interactions action, and then clench to touch it.
  Motion Pointer should be selected
- ❖ Clench once to activate the **Motion Pointer** feature
  You'll see a cursor on your display
- ❖ Tilt your smartwatch to position the cursor at the lower edge of your display to scroll down.
- ❖ Hold the cursor briefly over the Stopwatch application to launch it.
- ❖ Hold the cursor over the start button to touch it.
- ❖ To go back to the watch face, simply clench twice to display the Actions Menu, pinch to choose the Press Crown action, and then clench once to touch it.

Use quick actions

The **Quick Actions** feature helps you to respond when your smartwatch displays an alert. For instance, if you have an incoming call, a prompt will inform you that you can pinch twice to answer the call. The **Quick Actions** feature can also be used to stop a timer, begin a workout when your smartwatch detects a workout, snap a picture when the Shutter & viewfinder are showing in the Camera application, and snooze an alarm. To activate or deactivate Quick Actions, simply adhere to the directives below:

❖ Enter the Settings application on your smartwatch.
❖ Head over to Accessibility> Quick Actions, and then select one of the options.
   Tip: Touch the **"Try it out"** button to practice the quick action gestures.

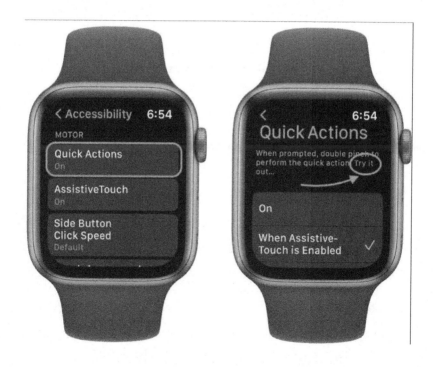

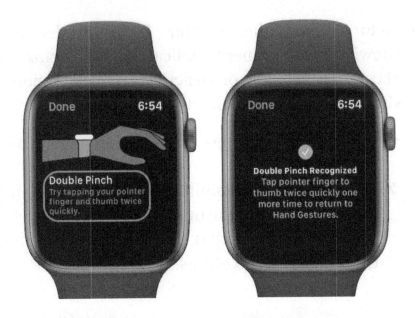

Change AssistiveTouch settings

Adjust the actions assigned to Motion Pointer gestures, clench, & pinch, and also change the Motion Pointer sensitivity.

Enter the Settings application on your smartwatch, head over to Accessibility, touch AssistiveTouch, and then carry out any of the below:

❖ Personalize gestures: Touch the **Hand Gesture** button, touch one of the gestures, and then select one of the actions or a Siri shortcut.

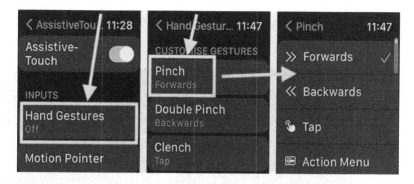

❖ Adjust the Motion Pointer: Touch the **Motion Pointer** button, and then change the sensitivity settings, hot edges, movement tolerance, & activation time.

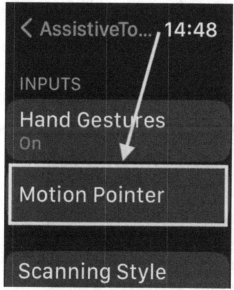

❖ Scanning style: Select one of the scanning modes (Manual or Automatic). The Automatic mode helps your watch to automatically highlight actions one after the other, while in

Manual mode, you have to use gestures to switch between actions.

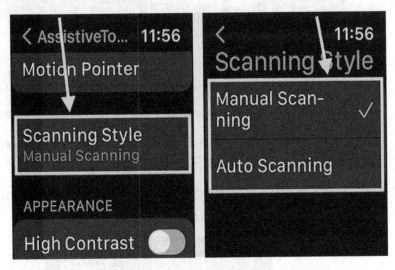

❖ Appearance: Activate the **High Contrast** to enhance features. Click on the **Colour** button to select another highlight colour.

❖ Personalize Menu: Make changes to the auto-scroll speed, change the size & position of the Actions Menu, & more.

❖ Confirm with AssistiveTouch: Enable this feature to be able to use the AssistiveTouch feature to verify payments with the password or whenever double-pressing the side button is necessary.

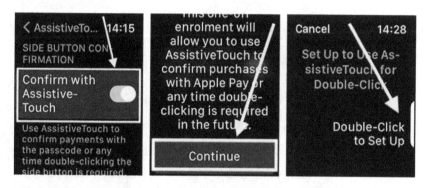

You can also enter the Watch application on your phone, touch the **My Watch** tab, and then head over to Accessibility> AssistiveTouch.

Use zoom on your smartwatch

You can use **Zoom** to make things bigger on your watch's screen

Activate Zoom

❖ Enter the Settings application on your smartwatch.

❖ Head over to Accessibility> Zoom, and then activate the **Zoom** feature.

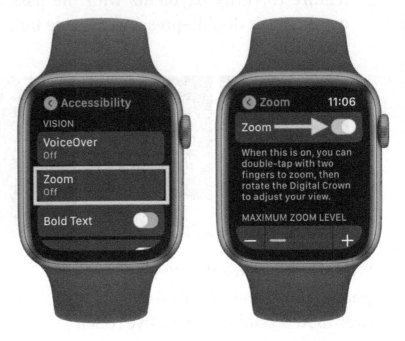

Or, enter the Watch application on your phone, touch the **My Watch** tab, touch Accessibility, and then touch Zoom.

Controlling Zoom

After activating Zoom, you can carry out the following actions on your smartwatch.

❖ Zoom: Use 2 fingers to double-tap your watch's screen to zoom in or out.

❖ Pan (Move around): Drag your watch's screen with 2 fingers. Or, rotate the Digital Crown to pan over the whole page, up-down & left-right. The small zoom icon that pops-up indicates where you're on the page.

❖ Return the Digital Crown to its default function: Tap your watch screen with 2 fingers to switch between using the Digital Crown to pan and using it for its default function. (For instance, scrolling through a list or zooming in on a map).

❖ Adjust zoom: Double-tap & hold with 2 of your fingers, and then slide your fingers down or up on your watch screen. Touch the minus or plus button on the Maximum Zoom Level slider to limit the zoom.

Tell the time on your Apple Watch using haptic feedback

When your smartwatch is in silent mode, it can use a set of unique taps to tap out the time on your wrist. Adhere to the directives below:

❖ Head over to the Settings application on your smartwatch.
❖ Touch the Clock button, scroll down, and then touch **Taptic Time**.
❖ Enable Taptic Time, and then select one of the settings—Morse code, Terse, or Digits. Minutes & hours are displayed in the following ways:

➢ Digits: Your smartwatch will long tap your wrist for every ten hours, short tap for every hour that follows, long tap for every ten minutes, and then short tap for every minute that follows.
➢ Terse: Your smartwatch will long tap your wrist for every 5 hours, short tap your wrist for the remaining hours, and then long tap you for each quarter hour.

- ➢ Morse code: Your smartwatch will tap each digit of the time on your wrist in Morse code.
- ❖ Hold down 2 fingers on the watch face to feel a haptic version of the time.

Or, setup Taptic Time on your phone. To do this simply enter the Watch application, touch the **My Watch** tab, head over to Clock> Taptic Time, and then activate it.

Change text size

- ❖ Press your watch's side button to reveal the Controls Centre.
- ❖ Touch the Text Format button AA, and then rotate the Digital Crown to change the size.

Make text bold

- ❖ Enter the Settings application on your smartwatch
- ❖ Touch Accessibility, and then activate Bold text

Live Speech

With the Live Speech feature, you can type & have your words spoken out loud, both in person or in calls.

Setup the Live Speech feature

❖ Enter the Settings application.
❖ Head over to Accessibility> Live Speech and then touch Voices.
❖ Select one of the voices, and then touch the **Speak Sample** button to listen to it.
To make use of the voice, simply touch the **Download [voice's name]** button and then touch the **Use Voice** button.
❖ To setup the accessibility shortcut to activate the **Live Speech** feature, enter the Settings application> Accessibility> Accessibility Shortcuts, then select the **Live Speech** option.

Type to speak

❖ Click the Digital Crown three times, and then type what you want your watch to say or select one of your favourite phrases.

Tip: Add your frequently used phrases for quick access. Enter the Settings application> Accessibility> Live Speech, and then touch Favourite Phrase.

❖ Click on the **Speak** button to make your watch read out the sentence.

Perform a quick calculation

❖ Enter the Calculator application .
❖ Click on the numbers & operators to get answers.

Split the check and calculate a tip

❖ Enter the Calculator application.
❖ Enter the total bill, and then click on the **Tip** button.

❖ Rotate the Digital Crown to select the tip percentage.

❖ Click on the **People** button, and then roll the Digital Crown to select the number of individuals that want to share the bill.

You'll see the total amount, the tip, and more on your screen.

SIRI

With Siri's help, you can perform tasks & receive answers to questions on your smartwatch. You can tell Siri to translate a sentence, set an alarm, find a place, and more.

Setup Siri

On your smartwatch, enter the Settings application, touch Siri, then activate the Raise To

Speak, Listen for Hey Siri, and Press Digital Crown feature.

How to use Siri

Carry out any of the below to make a Siri request:

❖ Raise your hand and talk to your smartwatch.
  To disable this feature, simply enter the Settings application on your smartwatch, touch the **Siri** button, and then disable the **Raise to Speak** feature.
❖ Say "Siri" or "Hey Siri" and then make a request.

To disable this feature, enter the Settings application on your smartwatch, touch Siri, touch Listen for "Hey Siri" or "Siri," and then touch the **Off** button.

❖ Long-press the Digital Crown till the listening indicator appears, and then ask for something.

To deactivate this feature, enter the Settings application on your smartwatch, touch Siri, and then disable the **Press Digital Crown** feature.

Tip: After activating Siri, you can put your hand down. Your watch will tap you when there is a response.

To answer Siri's question or continue the conversation, simply long-press the Digital Crown and talk

Note: To use Siri, your smartwatch has to have an internet connection.

Choose how Siri responds

Enter the Settings application on your smartwatch, touch the **Siri** button, touch Siri Response, and then select from the below:

- Always on: Siri will speak responses, even when you put your smartwatch in silent mode.
- Controls in silent mode: Siri's responses will be silenced when you put your device in silent mode.
- Headphones only: Siri will only speak responses when you connect your device to a Bluetooth headphone.

To change Siri's voice & language, enter the Settings application, touch Siri, and then touch Siri Voice or Language. After touching Siri Voice, you can now select from the available options.

Show captions & your Siri requests transcriptions

Your smartwatch can show Siri captions and transcription for Siri requests & Siri response. To make changes to any of the options, enter the Settings application, touch Siri, touch Siri Response, scroll, and then activate or deactivate Always Show Siri Caption & Always Show Speed.

Type to Siri

You can use Siri without speaking. Adhere to the directives below to type your request instead of speaking it.

❖ Enter the Settings application
❖ Head over to Accessibility, touch Siri, and then activate the **Type to Siri** feature.

Set how long you want Siri to wait for you to finish talking

❖ Enter the Settings application
❖ Head over to Accessibility, touch Siri, scroll down, and then select one of the options under Siri Pause Time.

Delete Siri's history

Your Siri requests are stored on Apple's servers for 6 months to make Siri's responses to you better. You can erase these requests at any time.

❖ Enter the Settings application
❖ Touch Siri, touch Siri History, and then touch Delete Siri History

Announce Notifications

Siri can read out notifications from many applications when you are making use of supported Airpods & headphones.

❖ Pair your headphone with your smartwatch and put it on.
❖ Enter the Settings application
❖ Head over to Siri> Announce Notifications, and then activate the **Announce Notification** feature.

Or, enter the Settings application on your phone, head over to Notifications> Announce Notification, and then activate the **Announce Notification** feature.

Tip: You can also tell Siri to help you read out your unread notifications in the Notifications Centre. To do this, simply say **"Read my notifications "**.

Select applications for notification

You can select which applications are allowed to announce notifications.

- ❖ Put on your connected headphones
- ❖ Enter the Settings application on your smartwatch.
- ❖ Head over to Siri> Announce Notification, scroll down, and then select the applications.

Temporarily disable the Announce Notifications feature

- ❖ Press your watch's side button to reveal the Controls Centre
- ❖ Touch the Announce Notifications button

Touch the Announce Notifications button once more to activate it.

Stop Siri from reading a notification

Carry out any of the below:

- ❖ You could say **Cancel** or **Stop.**
- ❖ Press the Digital Crown.
- ❖ Double tap one of the AirPods
- ❖ Press the Force Sensor on the AirPod

Announce calls

The Announce Calls feature allows Siri to identify incoming calls, which can be declined or accepted with your voice.

- ❖ Enter the Settings application
- ❖ Touch the **Siri** button, and then activate the **Announce Calls** feature.
- ❖ When someone calls you, your watch will identify the caller and ask if you would like to take the call. You can either say Yes to take the call or No to reject it.

SAFETY FEATURES

Your smartwatch can be useful in emergencies.

Setup & view your Medical ID

Your Medical ID contains info about you that can be important in emergency situations, such as health conditions & allergies. When you setup your Medical ID in the Health application on your phone, that info will become available on your smartwatch. If you share your medical ID, your smartwatch can send your medical info to the emergency department when you use Emergency SOS or contact 911.

Your smartwatch can display your Medical ID so that the person who attends to you in an emergency can easily see it.

Adhere to the directives below to view your Medical ID on your smartwatch:

❖ Long-press the side button till you see the sliders
❖ Drag the Medical ID slider to the right end of the screen

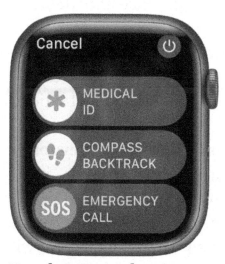

❖ Touch **Done** when you are done.

Or, enter the Settings application, then head over to SOS>Medical ID.

Setup Medical ID & add emergency contacts

❖ Enter the Settings application on your phone, then touch Health> Medical ID
❖ Click on the **Edit** button.
❖ Insert your birthdate and other health info.

❖ Touch the Add icon ➕ in the Emergency Contacts section to add emergency contacts. Touch one of the contacts, and then add their relationship to you.
❖ To remove a contact, simply touch the Remove icon ➖ beside the contact and then click on the **Delete** button.
❖ Activate the **Show When Locked** option to make your health info accessible from the lock screen. In an emergency situation, this provides info to individuals that want to help. Activate the **Share during Emergency Call** option to share your health info with emergency personnel. When you call or text emergency services on your phone or smartwatch, your Medical ID will be automatically shared with the emergency department.

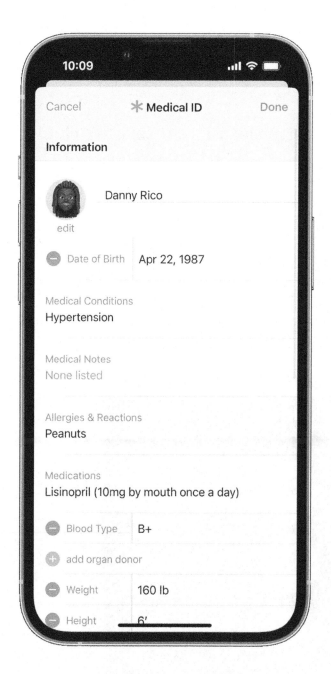

❖ Click on the **Done** button.

Contact emergency services on your Apple Watch

In an emergency, use your smartwatch to call for help.

Contact emergency services

Carry out any of the below:

❖ Long-press the side button till you see the sliders, and then drag the Emergency Call slider to the right end of the screen

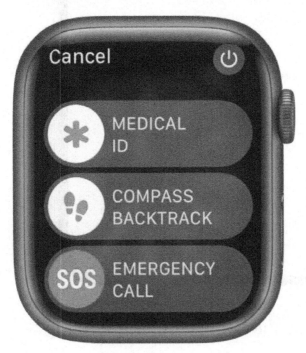

Your smartwatch will call the emergency department in your area, such as 911 (In some areas, you may have to press a number on the keypad to complete the call.)

❖ Say **Hey Siri call 911**
❖ Long-press the side button till your smartwatch displays a warning sound & begins a countdown. When the countdown is complete, your smartwatch will call the emergency department. Your smartwatch will make the warning sound even if you put it in silent mode, so if you are in an emergency and do not want to make a sound, use the emergency call slider.

If you do not want your device to automatically begin the countdown when you long-press the side button, simply disable the **Automatic Dialing** feature. To do this, just enter the Settings application, touch SOS, touch **Hold Side Button**, and then disable Hold Side Button.

End emergency calls

Touch the End Call icon , and then touch the **End Call** button to cancel.

Update your emergency address

If the emergency department cannot find your exact location, they will go to your emergency address.

- ❖ Enter the Settings application on your phone.
- ❖ Head over to Phone> WiFi Calling, touch Update Emergency Address, and then fill in your emergency address details.

Fall Detection

With Fall Detection activated, your smartwatch can help you contact the emergency department and send notifications to your emergency contacts if it detects a serious fall. If your smartwatch notices a serious fall & that you haven't moved for a minute or so, it will tap your hand, play an alarm, and then try to contact the emergency department.

To contact the emergency department, your smartwatch or iPhone needs a mobile connection.

If the date of birth you entered when setting up your smartwatch shows that you are fifty-five years old or older, Fall Detection is activated automatically. If you are between the ages of eighteen & fifty-five, you can manually activate Fall Detection by adhering to the directives below:

❖ Launch the Settings application on your smartwatch.
❖ Head over to SOS> Fall Detection, and then activate the **Fall Detection** feature.
  Or, enter the Watch application on your phone, touch the **My Watch** button, touch the Emergency SOS button, and then activate the **Fall Detection** feature.

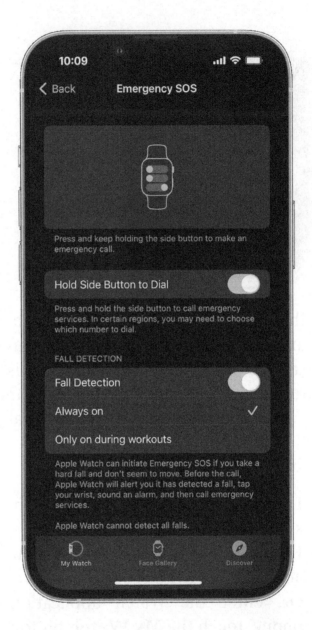

Note: If you deactivate the **Wrist Detection** feature, your smartwatch will not automatically try to contact emergency services even if it detects a serious fall.

❖ Select "Always on" or "Only during workouts"

Crash Detection

If your smartwatch detects a serious car accident, it can help you contact emergency services and alert your emergency contacts.

When your smartwatch notices a serious car accident, it'll show an alert & automatically begin an emergency call after twenty seconds unless you cancel. If you're unresponsive, your watch will play a voice message for the emergency department, telling them that you have been involved in a serious car accident. It will also send your location details to emergency services.

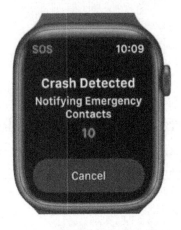 

To contact the emergency department, your smartwatch or iPhone needs a mobile connection.

If mobile network is not available, and your iPhone 14 or later is close to your smartwatch, it will try to send the Crash Detection notifications to emergency services using Emergency SOS via satellite system.

Activate or deactivate Crash Detection

❖ Enter the Settings application
❖ Head over to SOS> Crash Detections, and then deactivate **Call After Severe Crash**.

WATCH FACES

Your smartwatch comes with a collection of watch faces that can be customized to suit your style.

Visit the Apple Watch face gallery

You can find all your Apple Watch faces in the Face gallery. If you see the one you like, you can personalize it, select complications, and then add it to your collection.

Open the Face Gallery

Enter the Watch application on your phone, and then touch the **Face Gallery** tab at the lower part of your display.

Select features for a watch face

In the Face gallery, touch one of the watch faces, and then touch one of the features like style or colour.

Add complications

❖ In the Face gallery, touch one of the watch faces, and then touch one of the complication positions, like Bottom, Bottom Left, etc.

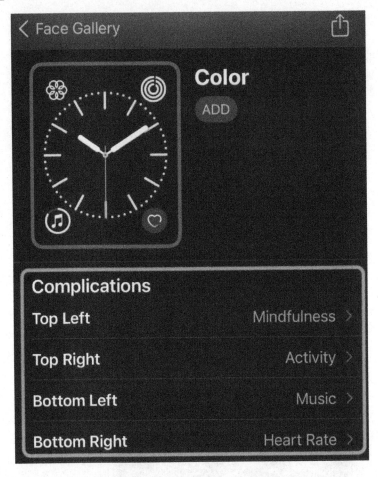

❖ Swipe to view available complications for the position you chose, then touch one of them.

- ❖ If you decide you do not want the position to have any complication, simply scroll up and touch the **Off** button.

Add a face

- ❖ In the Face gallery, touch one of the faces, and then select the complications & features you like.
- ❖ Click on the Add button.

The watch face will be added to your collection & it will become your current Apple Watch face.

Personalize the watch face

You can customize your watch face—right on your Apple Watch—to look the way you like & provide the features you want.

Pick another watch face

Long-press the watch face, swipe to find the one you like, and then touch it.

Swipe left or right to see other watch faces.

Simple

Edit — Add features to your watch face.

Add a complication to the watch face

You can add features known as complications to some of your Apple watch faces, so that you can easily check the price of a stock, the weather forecast, and more (you can launch a lot of applications by touching a complication on your watch face).

* ❖ With the watch face showing, long-press your screen, and then click on **Edit**.
* ❖ Swipe left continuously till you get to the end.
  If a watch face has complications, you'll see them on the last screen.
* ❖ Touch one of the complications to select it, and then rotate the Digital Crown to choose another complication—like Music or Workout.

* ❖ When you are done, press the Digital Crown to store the changes you've made, and then touch the face to start using it.

Add a watch face to your collection

❖ With the watch face showing, long-press your screen.

❖ Swipe left continuously till you get to the end, and then touch the Add icon (+).

❖ Rotate the Digital Crown to view the watch face, and then touch the **Add** button.
After adding it, you can personalize the watch face.

Tap new, scroll to browse watch faces, then tap a face to add it.

Check out your collection

You can view all your watch faces at once.

❖ Enter the Watch application on your phone.
❖ Touch the **My Watch** tab, and then swipe to see your collection in the My Faces section.

To reorder your collection, touch the **Edit** button in the **My Faces** section, then drag the Reorder icon  beside a watch face down or up.

Delete a watch face from your collection

❖ With the watch face showing, long-press your screen.
❖ Swipe to the watch face you want to delete, swipe the watch face up, and then touch the **Remove** button.

Swipe up to delete a watch face, then tap Remove.

Or, enter the Watch application on your phone, touch the **My Watch** button, and then touch the **Edit** button in the My Faces section. Click on the Delete icon ⊖ beside a watch face, and then touch the **Remove** button.

Set the watch ahead

❖ Enter the Settings application.
❖ Click on the **Clock** button

❖ Touch +0 min, and then rotate the Digital Crown to set your watch ahead.

This setting only changes the time displayed on your watch face—it does not have any effect on alarms, notifications, or other times (like the World Clock).

Share Apple Watch faces

You can share watch faces with your friends.

❖ With the watch face showing, long-press your screen, and then touch the Share button .

❖ Touch the watch face's name, then touch the **Don't include** button for the complications you do not want to share.

❖ Touch one of the recipients, or touch Mail or Message
If you select Mail or Message, add a contact & message

❖ Touch the **Send** button.

Or, enter the Watch application on your phone, touch one of the watch faces from Face Gallery or your collection, touch the Share icon ⬆, and then select one of the sharing options.

Receive a watch face

- ❖ Open an e-mail, link, or text that contains the watch face that was sent to you.
- ❖ Touch the watch face, and then touch the **Add** button.

Create a photo watch face

While viewing a picture in the Photos application ✻, click on the Share icon ⬆, scroll down, and then click on the **Create Face** button.

ACTIVITY

The Activity application tracks your activity throughout the day and prompts you to reach your fitness goals. The application tracks how often you stand, how long you exercise, & how much you move. 3 different colored rings summarize your progress. The goal is to complete each ring every day by sitting less, moving more, and exercising.

The Fitness application on your phone records your activity. If you have tracked activity for a minimum of 6 months, the Fitness application will show daily trend data for active calories, walking pace, cardio fitness, stand hours, walk distance, standing minutes, exercise minutes, standing hours, etc. In the Fitness application on your phone, touch the **Summary** tab, then go to Trends to view how you are doing compared to your usual activity.

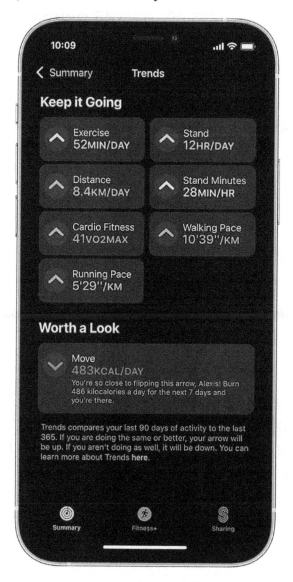

Getting started

When setting up your smartwatch, you are asked if you would like to setup the Activity application. If you decide not to set it up, you can configure it when you launch the application for the 1st time on your smartwatch.

❖ Enter the Activity application.
❖ Use the digital crown to read the Stand, Exercise, & Move descriptions, and then touch the **Get Started** button.

View your progress

Enter the Activity application to check your progress. The application will display 3 rings.

❖ The red activity ring shows the amount of calories you have burned.
❖ The blue one shows how many times in a day you have stood & moved for a minimum of 1 minute per hour.
❖ The green one displays how many minutes of brisk activity you have done.

If you've indicated that you're using a wheelchair, the blue stand ring changes to a Roll ring and shows how many times you have rolled at least 1 minute per hour.

Rotate the Digital Crown to view your current total—keep scrolling to see activity history, your total distance, and more.

When a ring overlaps, it means that you have exceeded your target. Touch the Weekly Summary icon  to see the summary of your activity for the week

Check your weekly summary

❖ Enter the Activity application.

❖ Click on the Weekly Summary button .

Change your goals

❖ Enter the Activity application.

❖ Click on the Weekly Summary button .

❖ Roll the Digital Crown to scroll down, and then touch the **Change Goals** button.

❖ Touch the Add icon or the Minus icon to make adjustments to a goal, and then touch the **Next** button.

❖ Touch **OK** when you are done.

To adjust the targets for each ring, rotate the Digital Crown to any of the rings and then click on the Change Targets button .

View your activity history

❖ Enter the Fitness application on your phone, and then touch the **Summary** tab.

❖ Touch the Activity area, click on the Calendar button ، and then click on a date.

Check your awards

You can get awards for personal bests, major milestones & steaks using your smartwatch. Adhere to the directions below to view your awards:

❖ Enter the Activity application.
❖ Click on the Awards button ⬭.
❖ Touch one of the awards to get more info about it.

View your meditation & workout history

You can see information about the meditations & workouts you have completed.

❖ Enter the Activity application.
❖ Scroll down till you get to the end of the screen.
❖ Touch one of the workouts or meditations to review it.

Control reminders

Reminders can help you achieve your goals. Your smartwatch can let you know if you are ahead or behind on your activity target. Adhere to the directives below to choose which alerts & reminders you want to see:

❖ Enter the Settings application on your smartwatch.
❖ Touch the **Activity** button, and then set the notifications

Or, enter the Watch application on your phone, touch the **My Watch** tab, and then touch Activity.

Stop daily coaching

Adhere to the directives below to disable activity reminders:

- ❖ Enter the Settings application on your smartwatch.
- ❖ Touch the **Activity** button, and then deactivate **Daily Coaching**

Or, enter the Watch application on your phone, touch the **My Watch** tab, touch Activity, and then deactivate Daily Coaching.

Share your activity with others

Share your activity with others (for example, a coach, trainer, friend, or family member) to keep your fitness routine on track. You can receive alerts when your friends reach their targets, complete exercises, etc.

Add or remove a friend

❖ Enter the Activity application.

❖ Click on the Share button .

❖ Touch the **Invite Friend** button, rotate the Digital Crown to scroll through your contact list, and then touch one of them.

If your friend has not accepted the invitation, touch the person's name in the Invites section of the Sharing screen, and then touch the **Invite Again** button.

See your friend's progress

❖ Enter the Activity application.

❖ Click on the Share button .

❖ Rotate the Digital Crown to scroll through your friends list

❖ Touch the name of your friend to view their stats.

Compete with your friends

Be active in some healthy competition. You can compete with a friend and earn points based on the amount of the Activity Rings that you close. You earn points for every percentage you add to your ring every day. The competition will last for seven days and you can earn 600 points per day for a maximum of 4200 points for the week. Whoever has the highest number of points at the end wins the competition. During the competition, your smartwatch will let you know if you are winning or behind your competitors.

❖ Enter the Activity application.

❖ Click on the Share button , and then touch the name of your friend.

❖ Scroll down, and then touch the **Compete** button

❖ Touch Invite[name of the person], and then wait for the individual to accept the challenge.

Or when you get a notification stating that your friend closed their ring or doubled their activity goal, you can scroll down and touch the **Compete** button.

You can also enter the Fitness application on your phone, click on the **Share** button, touch one of your friends in the list, touch the **Compete** button, and then touch Invite [name of the person].

Change your friend settings

Enter the Activity application, click on the Share button , touch any of your friends on the screen, scroll down, and then carry out any of the below:

❖ Remove the person: Touch the **Remove Friends** button.
❖ Touch the **Hide my Activity** button to hide your activity from the person.
❖ Touch the **Mute notifications** button to silent all notifications from the person.

MEASURE YOUR BLOOD OXYGEN LEVEL

You can use the Blood Oxygen application to measure the amount of oxygen that your red blood cells carry from your lungs to the other parts of your body. Having knowledge of how much oxygen your blood has can help you understand your overall health & well-being.

Most people have a 95-100 percent blood oxygen level. However, some individuals live a normal live with oxygen levels lower than 95 percent.

Note: The measurement from the Blood Oxygen application isn't intended for medical use.

Setup Blood Oxygen

❖ Head over to the Settings application.
❖ Click on the **Blood Oxygen** button, and then enable **Blood Oxygen Measurements**.

Measure the level of oxygen in your blood

The Blood Oxygen application  can measure your blood oxygen level periodically throughout the day if background measurement is on, but you can measure it whenever you want.

❖ Enter the Blood Oxygen application.
❖ Place your hands on a table or on your lap and ensure your wrist is flat and your smartwatch screen is facing up.

Ensure your smartwatch is not loose or too tight on your wrist.

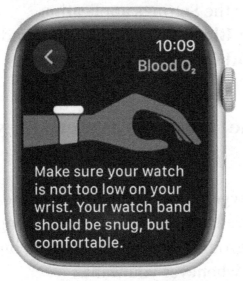

❖ Click on the **Start** button, and make sure your arm is still during the countdown.

The measurement takes about fifteen seconds.

❖ You will receive the results after the measurement is completed. Touch the **Done** button.

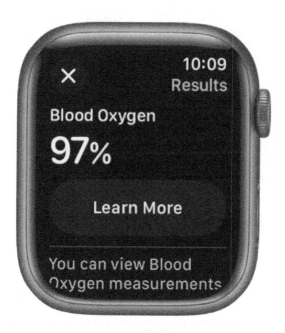

Disable background measurements when theater mode or the sleep focus is active

❖ Navigate to the Settings application.
❖ Click on the **Blood Oxygen** button, and then deactivate In Theater Mode & In Sleep Focus.

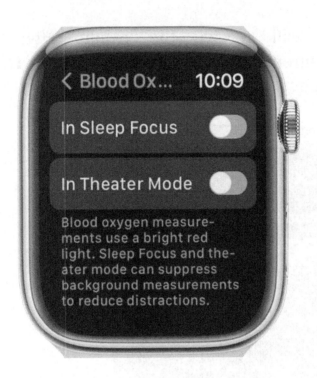

Check your blood oxygen measurement history

❖ Launch the Health application on your phone.
❖ Click on the **Browse** tab, click on Respiratory, and then touch the **Blood Oxygen** button.

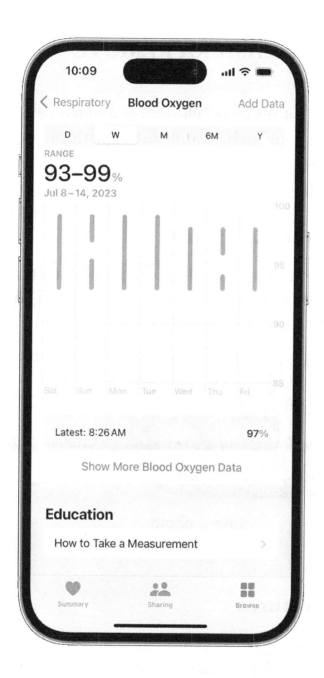

CAMERA REMOTE

You can set up your iPhone for a video or picture and use your smartwatch to snap the picture or record the video from a distance. There is a 3-second delay before your phone takes the picture or video, giving you time to put your hands done and get ready for the shot.

Note: Your smartwatch has to be within standard Bluetooth range of the phone (about 33ft) before it can function as a camera remote.

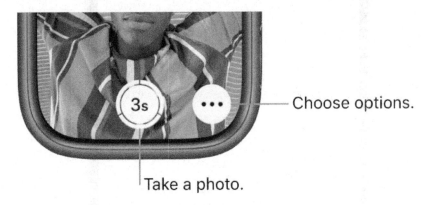

———— Choose options.

Take a photo.

Take pictures

❖ Launch the Camera Remote application on your smartwatch.

❖ Set your phone to take a photo with your smartwatch as the viewfinder.
Rotate the Digital Crown to zoom in & out. To change the exposure level, touch the main area of the shot in the preview image.

❖ Touch the Shutter to snap the picture

The pictures you capture will be stored in the Photos application on your phone, but you can review them on your smartwatch.

Record videos

❖ Launch the Camera Remote application on your smartwatch.

❖ Set your phone to record a video with your smartwatch as the viewfinder.
Rotate the Digital Crown to zoom in & out.

❖ Hold down the Shutter button to record the video

❖ Release the Shutter to stop the recording session.

Review your shots

Use the steps below to review your shots on your smartwatch.

❖ Touch the thumbnail in the lower left part of your display to view a picture.

❖ Swipe to the right or left to view other pictures
❖ Rotate the Digital Crown to zoom in or out.
❖ Fill your display: Tap the picture twice quickly.
❖ Touch your screen to hide or display the shots count & the Close button.

When you are done, click on the **Close** button.

Select another camera and change the settings

- ❖ Launch the Camera Remote application
- ❖ Touch the More Options icon ● ● ● , and then select from the options below:
  - ➢ Timer (activate or deactivate the 3-second timer)

  - ➢ Camera (choose the back or front camera)

➢ Flash (select off, on, or auto)

➢ Live Photo(select off, on, or auto)

COMPASS

The Compass application shows your watch's location, elevation, and the direction it's facing. You can save your location as a waypoint and then view the distance & direction to any waypoint you've created.

Choose a compass view

The Compass application has 5 views.

❖ When you launch the Compass application for the 1st time, you'll see your bearing in the middle of the watch face, with waypoints showing in the inner ring.

❖ Rotate the Digital Crown down to switch to the next compass view. In this view, you can find your heading at the lower part of the screen.

❖ Rotate the Digital Crown up 2 screens to switch to the next compass view. In this view, you will see your coordinates, elevation, & incline in the inner ring of the compass, and your bearing can be found on the outer ring. You'll see nearby waypoints in the middle.

❖ Keep rotating the Digital Crown to see the location of the waypoints that you've created and the waypoints that were automatically created to mark where you parked your vehicle, and give an estimate of the last place your smartwatch or phone could establish a mobile connection and where Emergency SOS was last available.

❖ Every screen that displays the compass dial has an Elevation icon in the lower edge of the screen. Touch the Elevation icon ⬤ to display a 3D view of the waypoint elevation based on your current elevation.

Show compass details

Enter the Compass application, and then touch the information button ⓘ in the upper left corner of your display to see coordinates (longitude & latitude), elevation, incline, & bearing.

View your waypoints

You can check out the waypoints that you have created in the Compass application.

❖ Enter the Compass application,

❖ Touch the information icon 🛈 in the upper left corner of your display, and then touch the **Waypoints** button.

❖ Click on Compass Waypoints to see the waypoints you have created and the ones that were automatically generated

Add a bearing

❖ Enter the Compass application

❖ Touch the Information icon 🛈 in the upper left corner of your display, and then touch the **Bearing** button

❖ Rotate the Digital Crowns to the bearing, and then touch the Mark icon ✅
To edit the bearing, touch the Information icon 🛈, scroll down, touch the **Bearing** button, rotate the Digital Crown to the new bearing, and then touch the Mark icon ✅

❖ To clear the bearing, touch the Information icon 🛈, scroll down, and then touch the **Clear Bearing** button.

Set a target elevation warning

If you set a target elevation, your smartwatch will notify you when you exceed the target so that you can rest & acclimate as you go.

❖ Enter the Compass application

❖ Touch the Information icon in the upper left corner of your display, and then touch the **Set Target Alert** button

❖ Rotate the Digital Crowns to select the target elevation.

To change the target, touch the Information icon, touch the **Target Alert** button, and then select a new target. To remove the target, touch the Information icon 🛈, and then touch the **Clear Target** button.

You'll receive a notification when your target elevation is exceeded.

Use true north

To use true north instead of magnetic north, simply adhere to the directives below:

❖ Enter the Settings application
❖ Touch the **Compass** button, and then activate the **Use True North** feature.

If a red spinning radar is shown on your display

If you see a red spinning radar screen when you enter the Compass application, it could be due to any of the below:

❖ Your smartwatch might be in a poor magnetic environment: The compass may be affected by magnetic materials in your watch band.

- ❖ Location Services is deactivated: To activate or deactivate Location Services, enter the Setting application, touch the **Privacy** button, and then touch Location Services.
- ❖ Compass Calibration is deactivated: To activate or deactivate the **Compass Calibration** feature, enter the Setting application on your phone, head over to Privacy & Security> Location Services, and then touch Systems Setting.

Create & show Compass Waypoints

You can add your location as a waypoint. You can then view the direction, distance, & elevation of every Waypoint you create.

- ❖ Enter the Compass application.
- ❖ Click on the Waypoint icon to add a waypoint.
- ❖ Fill in the waypoint info like colour, symbol (for example, cars or buildings), or label, and then touch the Mark icon .
- ❖ To see a Compass Waypoint, touch a waypoint on one of the 3 compass screens, rotate the

Digital Crown to choose a waypoint, and then touch the **Select** button.

Your screen will show the waypoint's direction, distance, & elevation—for example, "down 411ft."

❖ Touch the Edit icon ⬭ to change info about the waypoint you chose & to display the waypoint in a map with its coordinates.

Target a waypoint

Target a waypoint to see its direction, distance, & elevation.

❖ Enter the Compass application

❖ Touch the Information icon ⓘ, touch the **Waypoints** button, touch Compass Waypoints, and then touch one of the waypoints.

❖ Scroll down, and then touch the **Target Waypoint** button

Your screen will show the waypoint's direction, distance, & elevation

Use the Elevation dial

You can see waypoint elevations relative to your elevation.

❖ Enter the Compass application.

❖ Touch the elevation icon  in the lower part of your display.

Waypoints that are in your watch's direction are displayed with a column showing the elevation relative to your location. Waypoints that have Short columns are at lower elevations. A higher column indicates a higher elevation.

Retrace your steps with the Backtrack feature

With the Backtrack feature, you can track your path and then retrace your steps if you get lost.

❖ Enter the Compass application.
❖ Touch the Backtrack icon, and then touch the **Start** button to start recording your route.
❖ To retrace your steps, click on the "Pause" icon and then click on the **"Retrace Steps"** button.
You'll see where you first touch the Backtrack icon on the compass.
❖ Follow the path to go back to where you activated the **Backtrack** feature.
❖ When you are done, touch the Backtrack icon, and then touch the **Delete Steps** button.

CONTACTS & PHONE

In the Contact application, you can check out, edit, & share contacts from other devices using the same Apple ID with your smartwatch. You can also setup a contact card.

View contacts on your smartwatch

❖ Launch the Contacts application on your smartwatch.

- ❖ Rotate your watch's Digital Crown to scroll through the contacts list.
- ❖ Touch one of the contacts to see their photo, or scroll to view info like their work, & home address, e-mail address, etc.

To view your contact card, touch your profile photo in the upper right corner of your screen.

Connect with contacts

You can e-mail, send a text message, make a call, or start a Walkie-Talkie conversation right from the Contacts application.

❖ Enter the Contacts application.

❖ Rotate your watch's Digital Crown to scroll through your contacts list.

❖ Touch one of the contacts, and then carry out any of the below:

> ➤ Click on the Phone button 📞 to view the phone numbers of the contact. Touch one of the numbers to call it.

> ➤ Click on the Message button 💬 to start or continue a message conversation with the person.

> ➤ Click on the More options icon ⋯, and then click on the E-mail icon ✉ to compose an e-mail message.

> ➤ Touch the More Options icon ⋯, then touch the Walkie-Talkie icon 📻 to invite the individual to a Walkie-Talkie conversation or—if they have accepted your invitation & Walkie-Talkie is enabled on their device—start a Walkie-Talkie conversation.

Create a contact

❖ Enter the Contacts application.

- Click on the Add button ⊕.
- Type the name of the contact and add company (optional)
- Add a number, address, & e-mail, and then touch the Done icon ✓.

Share, block, edit, or delete contacts

- Enter the Contacts application.
- Rotate your watch's Digital Crown to scroll through your contacts list.
- Touch one of the contacts, scroll, and then carry out any of the below:
  - Touch the **Delete** button to delete the contact.
  - Touch the **Block Contact** button to block the contact.
  - Share the contact: Touch the Share icon 📤 at the lower right corner of your display, and then select one of the sharing options.
  - Edit the contact: Click the Edit button ✏, and then select the info you want to edit.

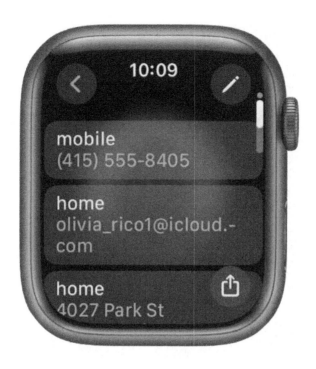

Answer a call

When someone calls you, lift your wrist to see who is calling.

❖ Decline the call: Touch the Reject button in the call notification.
❖ Take the call on your smartwatch: Touch the Answer button to speak your watch's inbuilt MIC & speaker or a Bluetooth device connected to your watch.

❖ Answer the call with your phone or send a message instead: Touch the More Options icon , and then touch one of the options. If you choose the **Answer on iPhone** option, the call will be placed on hold & the person calling will hear a repeating tone till you answer the call on your paired iPhone.

If you cannot find your phone, simply touch the Ping Phone button on your smartwatch.

While on a call

You can do any of the below while on a call:

❖ Transfer a call from your smartwatch to your iPhone: While talking on your smartwatch, unlock your phone, and then touch the line in the upper part of your display or the green button.

To quickly mute incoming calls, simply press your palm on your watch screen for 3 seconds. Make sure the **Cover to Mute** feature is activated — enter the Settings application on your smartwatch, touch Sounds & Haptics, and then activate the **Cover to Mute** feature.

❖ Change the volume of the call: Rotate the Digital Crown. Touch the Mute icon 🎤 to mute your device (for instance, if you are on a conference call).

❖ Insert additional numbers while on a call: Touch the More Options icon ⚫, touch the **Keypad** button, and then touch the digits.

❖ Transfer the call to an audio device: Touch the More Options icon ⚫, and select a device.

While on a Face-Time voice call, you can change the volume, touch the Mute icon 🎤 to mute the call, or touch the More Options icon ⚫ & select an audio destination.

Listen to a voicemail

If someone leaves a voicemail, your smartwatch will receive a notification—touch **Play** in the notification to listen to the voicemail. Or you can listen to it later, to do this, simply enter the Phone application on your smartwatch, touch the **Voicemail** button, and then choose the one you want to listen to.

Make a Call

❖ Enter the Phone application.
❖ Touch the Contacts button, and rotate the Digital Crown to scroll through the list.
❖ Touch one of the contacts, and then touch the **Phone** button.

❖ Touch the **Face-Time Audio** button to make a Face-Time voice call, or touch a phone number.

❖ Rotate the Digital Crown to change the volume while on the call.

Tip: To call somebody you have talked to recently, touch the **Recents** button, and then touch one of the contacts. To call someone you have added to your Favourites list in the Phone application on your phone, touch the **Favourites** button, and then touch one of the contacts.

Make a group FaceTime call

❖ Enter the Phone application on your smartwatch.

❖ Begin a Face-Time voice call.

❖ Carry out any of the below to invite more individuals to the call:

➢ Touch the More Options icon , touch the **Add People** button, and then select one of your contacts.

➢ If somebody has joined the call, touch the **2 People Active** button, touch the Add icon

 in the lower part of your display, and then select one of your contacts.

Enter a number on your smartwatch

❖ Enter the Phone application on your smartwatch.
❖ Begin a Face-Time voice call.
❖ Touch the More Options icon, and then touch the **Add People** button

Or, use the keypad to insert more digits while on a call. Simply touch the More Options icon ⬤ and then touch **Keypad**.

View call information on your watch

While talking on your phone, you can see the call details on your smartwatch in the Phone application and also end the call from your smartwatch.

CYCLE TRACKING

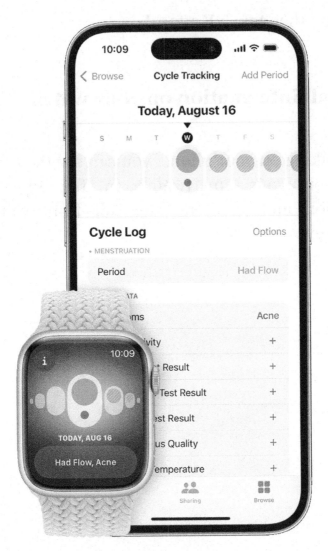

You can record details of your menstrual cycle in the Cycle Tracking application. You can add flow data & symptoms like cramps. With the info you have recorded, the Cycle Tracking application can predict when your fertile window or next period will begin. In addition to your input data, the Cycle Tracking application can utilize heart rate info to provide better predictions. If you wear your smartwatch to bed every night, the application can utilize your wrist temperature to enhance period forecast & provide ovulation predictions.

Setup Cycle Tracking

❖ Enter the Health application on your phone.
❖ Touch the **Browse** tab to enter the Health Category screen
❖ Touch the **Cycle Tracking** button
❖ Click on the **Get Started** button, and then adhere to the directives on your screen to set notifications & other options.

To remove or add more options after configuring Cycle Tracker, launch the Health application, touch the **Browse** tab, touch the **Cycle Tracking** button, and then Options beside Cycle Log.

Record your cycle

❖ Enter the Cycle Tracking application on your smartwatch.

❖ Carry out any of the below:
- ➢ Record a period on a specific day: With the date displayed on the timeline, click on the **Log** button. Click on the **Period** button, click the flow rate, and then click on the Done icon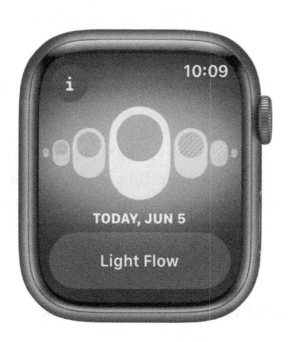.
- ➢ Record spotting, symptoms, & other info: With the date shown in the timeline, click on the **Log** button. Click on one of the categories, select an option, and then click on the Done icon.

The observations you recorded will be displayed in the cycle log on your phone. If you have activated Fertility Notifications & Period Notifications in the Health application on your phone, you'll get notifications on your smartwatch about retrospectives ovulation estimates, fertility window forecasts, & upcoming periods.

On your phone, you can also record factors in the Health application that may affect your cycle, which includes pregnancy, breastfeeding, & birth control. Depending on the factors you choose, retrospective ovulation estimates, fertility window forecast, & your period forecast may be deactivated on your phone & smartwatch.

Get retrospective ovulation estimates

When worn to bed every night, your smartwatch can track your temperature changes while you sleep & use this info to provide retrospective ovulation estimate & make period predictions better.

Setup wrist temperature tracking

- ❖ Setup Sleep monitoring(in the Sleep app) & Cycle Tracking
- ❖ To determine your temperature, make sure the Sleep Focus is activated, and then wear your smartwatch while you sleep.
  The Wrist temperature info will be available after 5 nights.
- ❖ To see the temperature info, launch the Health application on your phone, touch the **Browse** tab, touch the **Body Measurement** button, and then touch the **Wrist Temperature** button.

You should be able to see your retrospective ovulation prediction after 2 menstrual cycles of putting on your smartwatch to bed every night.

Deactivate the Wrist Temperature feature for Cycle Tracking

- ❖ Launch the Health application on your phone, touch the **Browse** tab, and then touch the **Cycle Tracking.**
- ❖ Scroll, touch Options, and then deactivate the **Use Wrist Temperature** feature.

ECG APP

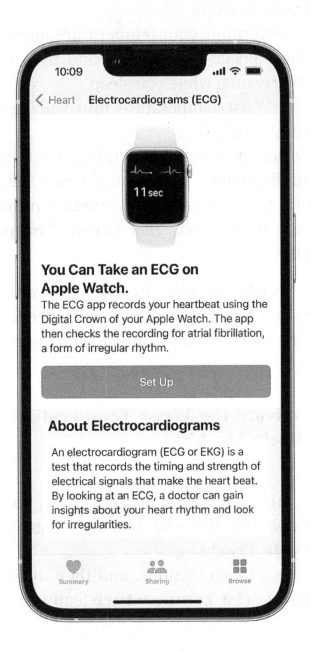

An ECG (also known as EKG or electrocardiogram) is a test that helps to record the intensity & timing of the electrical signals that cause the heart to beat. By observing an EKG, the doctor can get more knowledge of your heart rhythm & check for abnormalities.

The ECG application makes use of the electrical heart-sensor on your watch to record your rhythm & heartbeat and then checks the recording for AFib (a type of irregular rhythm).

The ECG application isn't designed for those under the age of 22.

Install & setup the ECG application

The ECG application 〰 is installed on your device when you configure it in the Health application. Adhere to the guidelines below to configure the ECG application:

❖ Head over to the Health application on your phone.
❖ Adhere to the guidelines on your display. If you do not see any setup prompts on your screen, touch the **Browse** tab in the lower part

of your display, then click on **Heart**> Electrocardiogram(ECG)> Setup ECG App.

❖ After you've finished setting up the app , enter the ECG application to take an ECG test.

If you still cannot find the application on your watch, launch the Watch application on your phone and click on the **Heart** button. Under ECG, click the **Install** button to install the ECG application.

Take an ECG

❖ Ensure your smartwatch is not too loose or tight & it's on the wrist you selected in the Watch application.

❖ Launch the ECG application

❖ Put your hand on your lap or a table

❖ Use a finger to hold the Digital Crown. You do not have to press your watch's Digital Crown while the test is going on

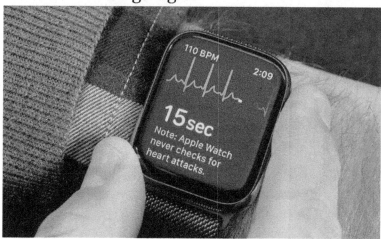

❖ Wait. The test will take about Thirty seconds. After the session, you'll get a classification, then you can click on **Add Symptoms** and select your symptoms.

❖ Click on the **Save** button to store any symptoms, then click on **Done**.

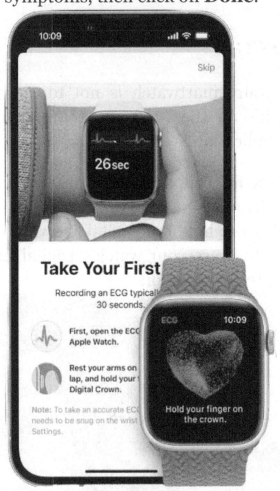

How to read the results

At the end of a session, you'll get one of the following results on the ECG application. Regardless of what the result is, If you are not feeling well you should see a doctor.

Inconclusive

When the result is inconclusive, it means the recording cannot be classified.

AFib

An Atrial fibrillation result implies that your heart is beating abnormally. Atrial fibrillation is a very common form of heart palpitations or arrhythmia.

Sinus rhythm

It means that your heart beats in a uniform pattern between 50 & 100BPM.

Low or high heart rate

In ECG version 1, a heart-rate that's below 50BPM or above 120BPM can affect the application's ability to check for Atrial Fibrillation. A heart-rate that's below 50BPM or above 150BPM in ECG version 2 affects the application's ability to check for Atrial Fibrillation

❖ A heart-rate can be high as a result of stress, Atrial fibrillation, infection, dehydration, exercise, alcohol, or other arrhythmias.
❖ A heart-rate could be low because of some medications or electric signals aren't conducted through the heart properly.

View & share your health info

The ECG Wave form, related classifications, and any noted symptoms will be stored in the Health application on your phone. You can also share the data in PDF format with a doctor.

❖ Head over to the Health application.
❖ Click on the **Browse** tab, touch Heart, and then click on Electrocardiogram (ECG).
❖ Click on chart to see your ECG results.
❖ Click on the **Export the PDF for your Doctors** option.

❖ Click on the Share icon 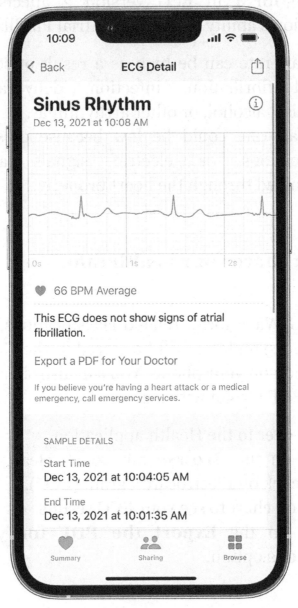 to share or print the file.

FIND PEOPLE

You can use the Find People application to know the location of your loved ones & also share your location with these individuals. If the person has an Apple Watch, iPad, or iPhone, and shares their location with you, you will be able to see where the person is on a map. You can set your watch to notify you when your friend leaves or arrives at a location.

Add a friend

❖ Launch the Find People application  on your smartwatch.

❖ Scroll down and then touch the **Share My Location** button.

❖ Touch the Keypad, Contacts, or Dictation button to select the friend

❖ Choose a phone number or e-mail address

❖ Select the duration— you can decide to share your location indefinitely, for 1 hour, or till the end of that day.

Your friend will be informed that you have shared your location with them. They may also choose to share their location too. After your friend has shared their location with you, you'll be able to see their location in a list or a map in the Find People application on your smartwatch or in the Find My application on your Mac, iPad, & iPhone.

If you want to stop sharing your location with someone, simply touch the name of the person in the Find People application, and then touch the **Stop Sharing** button.

If you want to stop sharing your location with everybody, simply enter the Settings application, head over to Privacy & Security, touch Location Services, and then deactivate the **Share My Location** feature.

Find your friend's location

❖ Enter the Find People application to see your friends list, with the location & distance of each friend from you. Rotate the Digital Crown to more people.

❖ Touch one of your friends in the list to see where they are on a map & their address.

❖ Click the Back button  to go back to the friends list.

Notify your friend of your arrival or departure

❖ Enter the Find People application.
❖ Touch one of your friends from the list, scroll down, and then touch the **Notify [friend's name]** button.

❖ Activate **Notify [friend's name]** on the next screen, and then choose to notify the person when you leave where you are or reach their location.

Receive an alert about your friend's location

❖ Enter the Find People application.
❖ Touch one of your friends from the list, scroll down, and then touch the **Notify Me** button.
❖ Activate the **Notify Me** feature, and then choose to receive a notification when your friend leaves where they are or reaches your location.

Receive directions to a friend

❖ Enter the Find People application.
❖ Touch a friend in the list, scroll down, and then touch the **Directions** button to launch the Maps application.

- ❖ Touch the route to receive directions from where you are to the current location of your friend.

Contact a friend

- ❖ Enter the Find People application.
- ❖ Touch a friend in the list, scroll down, touch the **Contact** button, and then touch a phone number or e-mail address.

FIND DEVICES & ITEMS

You can use the Find Device application to find your misplaced Apple device.

Activate the Find My network for your smartwatch

If your smartwatch is paired with your phone, it is automatically setup when you activate **Find My iPhone**. To locate your smartwatch even when it is disconnected or switched off, ensure Find My Network is enabled.

- ❖ Enter the Settings application on your smartwatch.
- ❖ Click on your name, and scroll down till you find your smartwatch.
- ❖ Touch your watch's name, and then touch the **Find My Watch** button.
- ❖ Activate the **Find My network** feature if it's not on.

See a device's location

If your device is online, you can find its location in the Find My Device application. For some Apple devices, the Find Devices application can find the device even when it is in Low Power Mode, switched off, or if Airplane Mode is activated.

Enter the Find Devices application on your smartwatch, and then touch one of the devices.

❖ If the application cannot find your device: You'll see **"No Location"** under the name of the device. In the Notifications section, activate **Notify When Found**. You'll be notified when the location becomes available.

❖ If the device can be found: It'll appear on the map so that you can view its location. The approximate distance to the device, when last it was connected to cellular or Wifi, & charge level will appear at the top of the map. You'll see the approximate location under the map.

Play a sound on your watch, Mac, iPad, or iPhone

❖ Enter the Find Devices application, and then touch the device you would like to play a sound on.

❖ Click on the **Play Sound** button.

> ➢ If the device is online: The sound will start playing and it will play for about 2 minutes. A "Find My Device" notification will appear on the screen of the device.
> ➢ If the device isn't online: Your screen will show **Sound Pending**. The sound will play the next time the device is connected to a WiFi or mobile network.

Play sound on your Beats headphones or AirPods

If your Beats headphone or AirPod is connected to your smartwatch, you can play a sound on them.

❖ Enter the Find Devices application, and then touch one of the devices on the list.

❖ Click on the **Play Sound** button.

> ➢ If the device is online: The sound will start playing and it will play for about 2 minutes.
> ➢ If the device isn't online: You'll be sent a notification the next time the device is close to your smartwatch

Receive directions to a device

❖ Enter the Find Devices application, and then touch the device you would like to receive directions to.
❖ Touch the **Directions** button to launch he Maps application.
❖ Touch the route to receive directions from where you are to the current location of the device.

Be notified when you leave a device behind

You can get notifications when you leave your device so you don't misplace it. You can also setup Trusted Places - places where you can leave your device without being notified.

❖ Enter the Find Devices application, and then touch the device you would like to setup a notification for.
❖ In the Notifications section, touch the **Notify When Left Behind** button, and then activate the **Notify When Left Behind** feature.

Or, launch the Find My application on your phone, touch the **Devices** button, touch the device you would like to set a notification for, and then touch the **Notify When Left Behind** button. Activate the **Notify When Left Behind** feature, and then adhere to the directives on your display.

To add a Trusted Location, simply choose one of the suggested locations, or touch the **New Location** button, choose a location on the map, and then touch the **Done** button.

Mark a device as lost

If you lost your device, you can activate Lost Mode or lock your Mac.

❖ Enter the Find Devices application
❖ Click on the Lost Mode button, and then activate the Lost Mode feature.

Here's what happens when you mark a device as lost:

❖ Apple Pay will be deactivated on the device

- ❖ You'll see the location of the device on the map.
- ❖ The device will not show alerts or make noise when it receives notifications
- ❖ A message will appear on the device's lock screen stating that the device is lost and how to reach you.
- ❖ A confirmation e-mail will be sent to your Apple ID e-mail address.

Locate an AirTag or other items

You can find a missing AirTag or 3rd-party item that you've registered to your Apple ID.

See an item's location

Enter the Find Items application on your smartwatch, and then touch one of the devices.

- ❖ If the application cannot find your device: You'll see when & where it was last found. In the Notifications section, touch the **Notify When Found** button, and then activate

Notify When Found. You'll be notified when the location becomes available.

❖ If the device can be found: It'll appear on the map so that you can view its location. The approximate distance to the device, when last it was connected to cellular or Wifi, & charge level will appear at the top of the map. You'll see the approximate location under the map.

Play a sound

If the item is close to you, you can play a sound to make it easier to find it.

❖ Enter the Find Items application, and then touch the item you would like to play a sound on.
❖ Click on the **Play Sound** button.
Touch the **Stop Sound** button to stop playing the sound before it stops by itself.

Receive directions to an item

You can receive directions to the present or last known location of an item.

❖ Enter the Find Items application, and then touch the item you would like to receive directions to.
❖ Touch the **Directions** button to launch he Maps application.
❖ Touch the route to receive directions from where you are to the current location of the item.

Be notified when you leave an item behind

You can get notifications when you leave an item so you don't misplace it. You can also setup Trusted Places - places where you can leave your item without being notified.

❖ Enter the Find Items application, and then touch the item you would like to setup a notification for.
❖ Touch the **Notify When Left Behind** button, and then activate the **Notify When Left Behind** feature.

Or, launch the Find My application on your phone, touch the **Items** button, touch the item you would like to setup a notification for, and then touch the **Notify When Left Behind** button. Activate the **Notify When Left Behind** feature, and then adhere to the directives on your display.

To add a Trusted Location, simply choose one of the suggested locations, or touch the **New Location** button, choose a location on the map, and then touch the **Done** button.

Mark a device as lost

If your AirTag or a 3rd-party item registered to your Apple ID is stolen or misplaced, you can activate Lost Mode.

- ❖ Enter the Find Items application, and then touch the item
- ❖ Click on the Lost Mode button, and then activate the Lost Mode feature.

If somebody finds the missing item, they can get more info about the item when they connect to it.

Deactivate Lost Mode

Deactivate Lost Mode when you find the item you misplaced

❖ Enter the Find Items application, and then touch the item
❖ Click on the Lost Mode button, and then deactivate the Lost Mode feature.

HEART

Your heart rate is a great way to monitor your body's health.

Check your heart rate

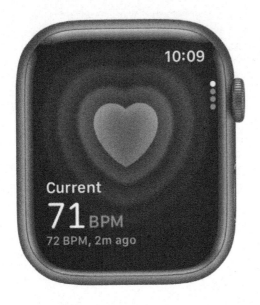

Enter the HeartRate application to see your heart rate at the moment, walking average rate, & resting rate.

Your smartwatch will continue to measure your heartrate as long as you wear it.

View your heart rate data graph

❖ Enter the Heart Rate application.
❖ Rotate the Digital Crown to Walking Average, Resting rate, & current Heart rate to see your heart rate for the day.

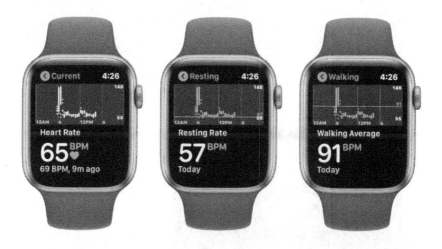

To view more heart rate data, enter the Health application on your phone, touch the **Browse** tab, touch the **Heart** button, and then touch an entry. You can view heart rate for the past year, month, week, day, or hour.

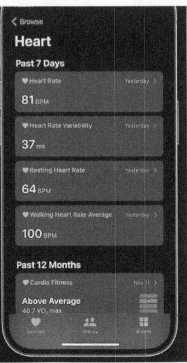

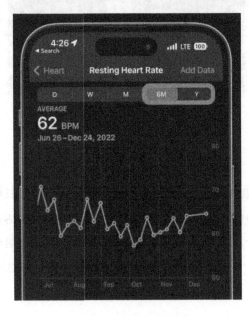

Activate heart rate data

If you have deactivated heart rate data, adhere to the directives below to reactivate it:

❖ Enter the Settings application on your smartwatch
❖ Head over to Privacy and Security> Health
❖ Touch the **Heart Rate** button, and then enable the **Heart Rate** feature

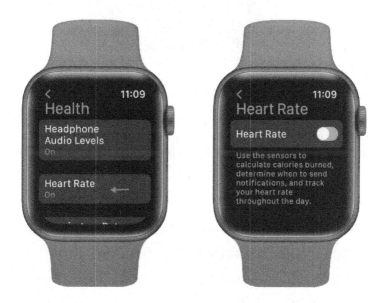

Or, enter the Watch application on your phone, touch the **My Watch** tab, touch the **Privacy** button, and then activate Heart Rate.

Get low or high heart rate alerts

❖ Enter the Settings application on your smartwatch, and then touch the **Heart** button
❖ Touch Low Rate Notifications or High Heart Rate Notification, and then select a heartrate limit.

Or enter the Watch application on your phone, touch the **My Watch** button, and then touch the **Heart** button. Click on Low Heart Rate or High Heart Rate, then set the limit.

Setup irregular heart rate alert

Your smartwatch will notify you if it detects an irregular heart rhythm like AFib.

- ❖ Enter the Watch application on your phone
- ❖ Touch the **My Watch** button, touch the **Heart** button, and then setup Irregular Rhythm Notification in Health
- ❖ In the Health application, touch Setup, and then adhere to the directives on your display.

MAIL

In the Mail application, you can read incoming messages, then reply with your watch, or switch to your iPhone to write a reply.

View an email notification

❖ When your smartwatch receives a notification, just lift your wrist to read the message.
❖ To dismiss the alert, touch the **Dismiss** button at the bottom of the message.

You can also swipe down from the top of the watch face to reveal the Notifications Center so that you can check if you have unread notifications.

To control mail notifications on your smartwatch, simply enter the Watch application on your phone, touch the **My Watch** button, and then head over to Mail> Custom

Read an email in the Mail application

❖ Enter the Mail application on your smartwatch.
❖ Touch one of the mailboxes, then rotate the Digital Crown to scroll down in the messages list.
❖ Touch one of the messages to read it
❖ Tap the top of your watch display to jump to the beginning of a long message.

Switch to iPhone

When your smartwatch receives a mail notification that you want to read on your phone, simply adhere to the directives below:

❖ Wake your iPhone.
❖ Swipe up from the lower edge of your screen & stop to display the Apps Switcher (For Face ID iPhone). Or, double-click the Home button to display the Apps Switcher (For Home-button iPhone)
❖ Click on the button in the lower part of your display to launch the Mail application.

Create a message

❖ Enter the Mail application on your smartwatch.
❖ Click on the New Message icon .
❖ Click on the **Add Contacts** button to add a recipient, click on **From** to select the account you want to send the e-mail from, click on **Add Subject** to write the title of the mail, and then touch the **Create Message** button.

Compose a message

You can write messages in different ways. Click on the Create Message field, and then do any of the below:

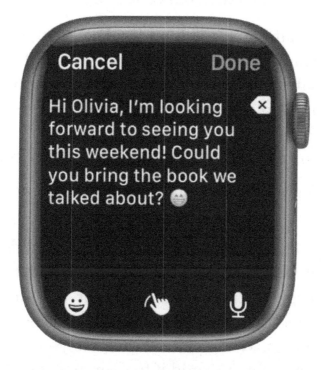

❖ Use the onscreen keyboard to type the message.
If you can't find the keyboard, simply swipe up from the lower edge, and then touch the **Keyboard** button.

❖ Using Scribble: Use a finger to write what you have in mind. To edit what you've written, rotate the Digital Crown to hover the cursor to the position, and then edit. To use Scribble, simply swipe up from the lower edge, and then touch the **Keyboard** button.

❖ Dictate text: Click on the Dictation icon 🎤, say what you want, and then touch the **Done** button. To insert punctuation, simply say the name of the punctuation mark,— for instance, "have you seen them question mark ".
To go back to using Scribble, simply rotate the Digital Crown or touch the Scribble icon 👆

❖ Add emoji: Touch the Emoji icon 😃, touch one of the frequently used emoji, or hold down one of the categories at the lower part of your display, drag to the right or left to select a category, and then scroll to see available emojis. When you see the one you are looking for, touch it to add it to your message.

❖ Type with your phone keyboard: When you start writing a message and your paired iPhone is near you, a notification will appear on your phone, offering to allow you to type text with your iPhone's keyboard. Touch the notification, and then type the message on your phone.

Reply to messages on your smartwatch

In the Mail app, scroll to the bottom of the message you received, and then touch the Reply icon ↰. If there is more than one recipient, click on the **Reply All** button. Then carry out any of the below:

❖ Send a smart reply: Scroll to check out a list of recommended phrases you could use - click on one of them to send it.

To add your own phrase to the list, simply enter the Watch application on your phone, touch the **My Watch** button, head over to Mail> Default Replies, and then touch the **Add Replies** button. Click **Edit** to edit custom responses, and touch the Delete icon ⊖ to erase one.

❖ Write a reply: Click on the Add Message field, and then write a reply.

Choose which mailbox appears on your smartwatch

❖ Launch the Watch application on your phone.
❖ Touch the **My Watch** tab, then head over to Mail> Include Mail
❖ Under Accounts, tap the accounts you would like to see on your smartwatch.
❖ If you like, touch an account, and then touch the specific Mailboxes to view their content on your smartwatch.

Delete a message

Touch the **Trash Message** button to delete the message.

If you are viewing the messages list, swipe the message to the left, and then touch the Trash icon 🗑.

MAPS

Use the Maps application to explore your surroundings & receive directions.

Use the Walking Radius

Walking Radius shows you places of interest in your surroundings.

❖ Enter the Maps application.
   The map will show a circle of places that you can walk to within minutes.
❖ Rotate the Digital Crown to adjust the radius.
   You can increase the radius to a walking time of 1 hour.

Search the map

❖ Enter the Maps application.

❖ Click on the Search icon , click the **Search** button, and then click the Dictate icon to dictate or the Scribble icon to type. You can also use your watch's onscreen keyboard.

Find a service near you

❖ Enter the Maps application.

- Click on the Search icon 🔍, click on the Search Places icon ⊞, and then click on one of the categories like Parking or Restaurants.
- Rotate the Digital Crown to surf through the results & see their location on the map
- Touch one of the results, and then rotate the Digital Crown to see info about it.
- Click on the Back button ◁ to go back to the results list.

Pan & zoom

- You can pan on the map by dragging one of your fingers around it.
- Rotate the Digital Crown to zoom in or out of the map.
  Or, double-tap the map to zoom in on a spot.
- Touch the Location icon ⏶ to return to your current location in the map.

Get directions on your smartwatch

The Maps application can provide directions for driving, biking, public transportation, & walking.

❖ Enter the Maps application.

❖ Touch the Search icon, then rotate the Digital Crown to go to Guides, Find Nearby, Recent, or Favourites.

❖ Click on an entry, touch a destination, and then touch the button in the upper right corner of your display to select cycling, public transport, walking, or driving directions.

❖ View an overview of the route: After you've started the journey, scroll up one screen to see where the route started. Touch the Overview icon in the upper right part of your display to see the whole route. Touch the Location icon to come back to your present location.

End directions

Touch the Cancel icon on a route, and then touch the **End Route** button.

USE MEMOJI

You can create your own Memoji—select the skin tone, hair colour & style, headwear, etc.

Create Memoji

❖ Enter the Memoji application.
❖ If this is your first time using the Memoji app, click on the **Get Started** button.
   If you have used the application to create a Memoji before, scroll up, and then touch the Add Memoji icon ⊕ to add a new one.

❖ Click on each feature & turn the Digital Crown to select your preferred Memoji option.

❖ Click on the Checkmark button to add it to your Memoji collection.

To create another one, touch the Add Memoji icon, and then add the features you want.

Edit Memoji & more

Enter the Memoji application, touch any of the Memoji, and then select one of the options:

- ❖ Edit a Memoji: Click on features like headwear & eyes, and then rotate the Digital Crown to select a variation.
- ❖ Duplicate a Memoji: Scroll down, and click on **Duplicate**.
- ❖ To create a Memoji watch face, simply scroll down, and then touch the **Create Watch Face** button.

  Go back to your watch face, and swipe left to check out the Memoji watch face you just created.
- ❖ To delete a Memoji, simply scroll down, and then click on the **Delete** button

MINDFULNESS

The Mindfulness application recommends taking a few minutes each day to focus, & connect with your breathing.

Begin a meditation or breathing session

Launch the Mindfulness application on your smartwatch, then carry out one of the below:

❖ Breathe: Click on **Breathe**, breathe in slowly as the animation gets bigger, and then breathe out as it starts getting smaller.

❖ Reflect: Click on **Reflect**, read the topic, focus, and then click on **Begin**.

To end a Breathe or Reflect session before it completes, swipe to the right, and click on **End**.

Set the duration of a session

❖ Launch the Mindfulness application  on your smartwatch
❖ Click on the More Options icon ●●●, click on **Duration**, and then select the duration.

You can choose between 1 minute & 5 minutes.

Change mindfulness settings

Launch the Setting application on your smartwatch, click on Mindfulness, then carry out any of the below:

❖ Set reminders: In the Reminders segment, enable or disable Start of Day & End of Day; click on the **Add Reminder** button to create more reminders.

❖ Receive or stop weekly summary: Activate or deactivate Weekly Summary.

❖ Change your breathing rate: Touch Breathe Rate to make changes.

❖ Receive new meditations: Activate the **Add a New Meditation to Watch** feature to download new meditations when your smartwatch is charging. The Meditations you have completed will be automatically erased from your smartwatch.

❖ Silent mindfulness reminder: Enable the **Mute for Today** feature

MUSIC

Add music to your smartwatch

After adding music to your smartwatch, you can listen to the songs anytime you want, even when you are not with your iPhone

Add music using your phone

❖ Launch the Watch application on your phone.
❖ Click on the **My Watch** button, and then touch the **Music** button.

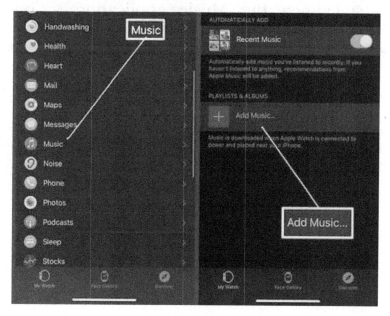

- ❖ In the Playlist and Albums section, touch the **Add Music** button.
- ❖ Choose playlist and albums to synchronize to your smartwatch, then touch the Add icon  to add them to the Playlist and Album queue.

Music will be added when your smartwatch is placed close to your phone.

Add music using your smartwatch

If you are an Apple Music subscriber, you can add songs with your smartwatch.

- ❖ Launch the Music application on your smartwatch.

❖ In the Listen Now screen, navigate to the song you would like to add
Or, from the Listen Now screen, touch the Back icon ◀ , click on the **Search** button, and then search for the song you want.

❖ Touch one of the albums or playlists, touch the More Options icon ⬤ , and then click on the **Add to Library** button.
An alert will appear confirming that the song has been added.
Note: You can stream the songs you've added to your smartwatch when you're connected to the Internet. If you want to play music offline, you'll need to download it first.

❖ If you want to download the song to your smartwatch, click on the More Options icon ⬤ once more, and then click on **Download**.

Add a workout playlist

You can add a playlist that will automatically start playing when you begin a workout in the Workout application on your smartwatch.

❖ Launch the Watch application on your smartphone.

- ❖ Click on the **My Watch** button, and then click on **Workout**.
- ❖ Click on **Workout Playlists**, and then select one of the playlists.

The playlists will be added to My Watch> Music in the Watch application on your phone.

Note that the workout playlist will not start playing if you are currently listening to other songs.

Remove music from your smartwatch

Note: To view how much music is saved on your smartwatch, head over to the Settings application on your smartwatch, click on General, then tap Storage. Or, launch the Watch application on your smartphone, click on the **My Watch** button, touch General, then touch Storage.

Remove music using phone

- ❖ Launch the Watch application on your phone.
- ❖ Click on the **My Watch** tab, click on Music, and then carry out any of the below:

➤ For the songs you added: Click on the **Edit** button, and then click on the Remove icon ⊖ beside the item you would like to remove.

➤ For songs that were automatically added: Deactivate Recent Music or other auto-added songs.

Songs you delete from your smartwatch will remain on your iPhone.

Remove music using your smartwatch

If you are an Apple Music subscriber, you can remove songs directly on your smartwatch.

❖ Launch the Music application 🎵

❖ From the Listen Now screen, touch the Back icon ◀, click on Library, scroll down, touch the **Downloaded** button, and then touch Albums or Playlist.

❖ Touch one of the albums or playlists, touch the More Options icon ⋯, and then click on **Remove**.

❖ Select the Remove Downloads or Delete from Library option.

Note: You can also delete individual songs. To do this, simply swipe a song to the left, click on the More Options icon , click on Delete from Library, and then touch the **Delete** button. The song will be removed from your smartwatch.

Play music on your watch

Tap for more options.

After connecting your smartwatch to a Bluetooth headphone or speaker, launch the Music application on your smartwatch, and then carry out any of the below:

❖ Play songs on your smartwatch: Rotate the Digital Crown to go through the Listen Now display, and then touch one of the albums, playlists, or categories.

❖ Play songs from your music library: From the Listen Now screen, touch the Back icon , click on Library, touch one of the categories like Downloaded, or Album, then select music.

❖ Search the Apple Music Library: Click on the **Search** button, enter a song, artist, or album, and then touch the **Search** button. Touch one of the results to play it.

NOISE

The Noise application  on your watch measures the sound level in your environment. When your smartwatch notices that the decibel level is high enough to affect your ears it can alert you with a tap on your wrist.

Setup the Noise application

❖ Launch the Noise application.

❖ Click on **Enable** to activate monitoring.

❖ In the future, launch the Noise application to measure the ambient noise around you.

Receive noise notifications

❖ Head over to the Settings application on your smartwatch.

❖ Click on Noise> Noise Notification, and then select any of the settings.

Or, enter the Watch application on your phone, touch the **My Watch** tab, touch Noise> Noise Threshold

Disable noise measuring

❖ Head over to the Settings application on your smartwatch.

❖ Click on Noise> Environmental Sounds Measurement, and then disable **Measure Sounds**.

Or, enter the Watch application on your phone, touch the **My Watch** tab, touch Noise, and then deactivate Environmental Sound Measurement

View noise notification details

You can receive an alert on your phone from your smartwatch when the noise around you gets to a level that can affect your ears.

To see the details of an alert, follow the directives below:

❖ Enter the Health application on your phone, and then touch the **Summary** button.
❖ Click on the notification close to the upper part of your display, and then click on the **Show More Data** button.

SLEEP

You can create a sleep schedule to help you achieve your sleep goals. Put on your smartwatch to bed, and it can track how much time you spend in each stage of sleep— Deep, Core, & REM—as well as when you wake up. When you wake up, launch the Sleep application to see how much sleep you've had & what your sleep patterns have been over the past fourteen days.

You can create more than one sleep schedule, for instance, one schedule for weekends & another sleep schedule for weekdays.

Setup sleep on your smartwatch

❖ Launch the Sleep application .
❖ Adhere to the directives on your display.

Or, enter the Health application on your phone, click on the Browse button, click on **Sleep**, and then click on **Get Started** in the Setup Sleep segment.

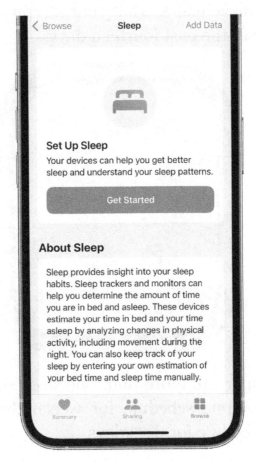

Change or turn off the next wakeup alarm

❖ Launch the Sleep application ⊖.

❖ Touch the Wake up Alarm icon ⏰.

❖ To set a new wakeup time, touch the wakeup time, rotate the Digital Crown to select a new time, and then click on the Done icon ✅.

Turn off Alarm if you do not want your smartwatch to wake you up in the morning.

Or, launch the Health application on your phone, click on the Browse button, click on the **Sleep** button, and then touch **Edit** under Your Schedule to adjust your schedule

This change only applies to your next wakeup alarm, after which your normal routine will resume.

Change or add a sleep schedule

❖ Launch the Sleep application.
❖ Rotate the Digital Crown scroll to Full Schedule, and then carry out one of the below:
  ➢ Touch the current sleep schedule to edit it
  ➢ Click on the **Add Schedule** button to add a sleep schedule.
  ➢ Change your sleep target: Click on the **Sleep Goals** button, then set your sleep duration
  ➢ Make changes to wind-down time: Click on the **Wind Down** button, and then set how long you want the Sleep Focus to be on before you fall asleep.
❖ Carry out any of the below:

➢ Set your schedule days: Click on your schedule, and then click Active On. Select days, and then click on the Back icon ⬤.

➢ Change your bedtime & wakeup time: Click on your schedule, click on Wakeup or Bedtime, roll the Digital Crown to select a new time, and then click on the Confirm button ⬤.

➢ Set alarm options: Click on your schedule, then deactivate or activate Alarm and touch Sounds & Haptic to select an alarm sound.

➢ Delete or cancel a schedule: Click on your schedule, and then click on the **Delete Schedule** button at the lower part of the screen to remove a schedule, or click on the **Cancel** icon ⬤ to cancel creating a new schedule.

Check out your sleep history

Enter the Sleep application ⬤ to check out how much sleep you had in the previous night, how long you spent in the different sleep phase & your sleep average over the past fourteen days.

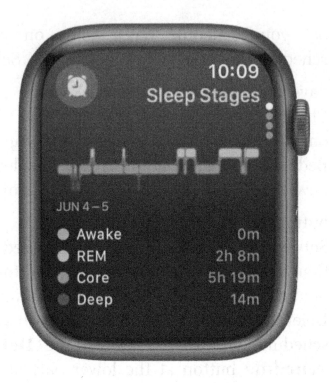

Check your sleep respiratory rate

Your smartwatch can monitor your breathing rate while you sleep, which can give you more insight into your overall well-being. After putting on your smartwatch to bed, follow the directives below:

❖ Launch the Health application on your phone, click on the **Browse** button, and then click on the **Respiratory** button.

❖ Click on Respiratory Rate, and then click on Show Respiratory Rate Data.
The sleep entry will show the range of your respiratory rate when you were asleep.

Turn off respiratory rate measurements

❖ Enter the Settings application on your smartwatch
❖ Head over to Privacy and Security> Health
❖ Touch the **Respiratory Rate** button, and then deactivate Respiratory Rate.

Or, enter the Watch application on your phone, touch the **My Watch** tab, touch Privacy, and then deactivate Respiratory Rate.

Monitor your nightly wrist temperature

When worn to bed every night, your smartwatch can monitor your wrist temperature changes every night to get more information about your well-being.

Setup wrist temperature tracking

❖ Turn on Track Sleep with Apple Watch (in the Sleep application)
   Or, head over to the Watch application on your phone, touch the **My Watch** button, touch the **Sleep** button, and then touch **Track Sleep with Apple Watch** to turn on this feature.
❖ To set a temperature baseline, make sure Sleep Focus is activated, then wear your smartwatch while you sleep.
   Wrist temperature info will become available after 5 nights.

Review your wrist temperature

❖ Launch the Health application on your phone, then click on the **Browse** button
❖ Click on Body Measurement, then click on Wrist Temperature
❖ Touch a point in the chart to view sample details

Disable wrist temperature tracking

❖ Enter the Settings application

❖ Head over to Privacy and Security> Health
❖ Touch Wrist Temperature, and then deactivate Wrist Temperature.

Or, enter the Watch application on your phone, touch the My Watch tab, touch the Privacy button, and then disable wrist Temperature.

VOICE MEMOS

You can record personal notes with the Voice Memos application.

Record a voice memo

❖ Enter the Voice Memos application.

❖ Click on the Record button ⚪.

❖ Click on the Stop Recording button ⚫ to stop recording.

Play a voice memo

* Enter the Voice Memos application
* Touch one of the recordings on the voice Memo screen, and then touch the Play button  to play it.
* To move forward or backward, click the Forward button or Backward button.
* To rename or delete the recording, simply click on the More Options icon , and then click on the **Edit Name** or **Delete** button.

WALKIE-TALKIE

Walkie-Talkie is an easy way to communicate with other Apple Watch users. Just like a real walkie-talkie, you press a button to speak and release the button to listen to the other person's response. The Walkie-Talkie requires both participants to be connected to a WiFi network, iPhone, or cellular connection.

Invite friends to use Walkie-Talkie

❖ Launch the Walkie-Talkie application .

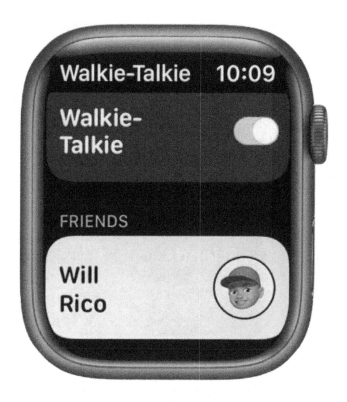

❖ Scroll through your contact list, and then click on one of the names to send an invitation.

When somebody accepts your invitation, you can begin a Walkie-Talkie conversation.

To add other people, touch the **Add Friends** button on your Walkie-Talkie screen, and then select one of the contacts.

Have a Walkie-Talkie conversation

❖ Launch the Walkie-Talkie application.
❖ Click on the name of your friend.
❖ Hold-down the Talk button and start talking.

If the friend you're trying to reach has made themselves available, the Walkie-Talkie application will open on their watch and they will hear what you said.

Rotate the Digital Crown to change the volume while talking.

Talk with one tap

If you have trouble long-pressing the Talk button, you can use a single tap to speak.

❖ Launch the Settings application.
❖ Click on **Accessibility**, and then enable **Tap to Talk** in the Walkie-Talkie segment.

After activating this feature, touch the button to talk, and then touch it one more time when you are done talking.

Or, enter the Watch application on your phone, touch the **My Watch** button, touch Accessibility, and then activate the Tap to Talk feature in the Walkie-Talkie section.

Accept Walkie-Talkie invitations

Click on **Always Allow** in the notification that pops up on your display when somebody sends you an invitation.

Remove contacts

In the Walkie-Talkie application on your smartwatch, swipe a contact to the left and then click on **X**.

Make yourself unavailable

❖ Press your watch's side button to reveal the Controls Centre
❖ Scroll down, and then click on the Walkie-Talkie button  .

Or, open the Walkie-Talkie application, scroll to the top of your display, and then disable Walkie-Talkie.

APPLE PAY

Apple Pay provides a safe, simple, & private way to make payments from your smartwatch.

Add cards to your smartwatch with your iPhone

* Enter the Watch application on your phone.
* Click on the **My Watch** tab, and then click on **Wallet and Apple Pay**.
* If you have a card on another Apple device or a card you recently removed, click on the **Add** button beside the card you would like to add, and then type the CVV of the card.
* For other cards, click on the **Add Card** button and then adhere to the directives on your display.

Your card provider may ask for more steps to verify your information.

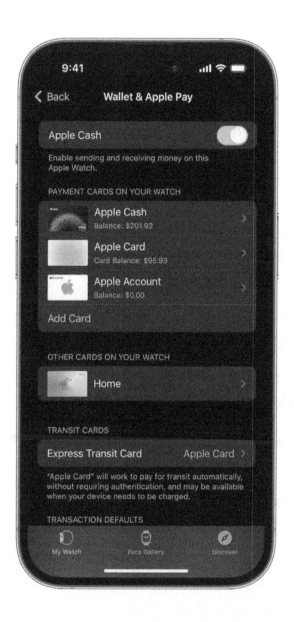

Add a card on your smartwatch

❖ Enter the Wallet application on your smartwatch.

❖ Click on the More Options icon⬤ , then click on the **Add Card** button.

❖ Select the card type, and then adhere to the directives on your display.

Pick your default card

❖ Enter the Wallet application on your smartwatch.

❖ Click on the More Options icon⬤ , click on the **Default Card** button, and then select one of the cards.

Remove a card from Apple Pay

❖ Enter the Wallet application on your smartwatch.

❖ Touch to select one of the cards

❖ Scroll down, and then click on the **Remove** button.

Change the default transaction info

You can change your transaction information in the app, including your phone number, e-mail, shipping address, & default card.

❖ Enter the Watch application on your phone.
❖ Touch the **My Watch** button, touch the **Wallet and Apple Pay** button, and then scroll to the Transaction Defaults section.
❖ Touch one of the items to edit it.

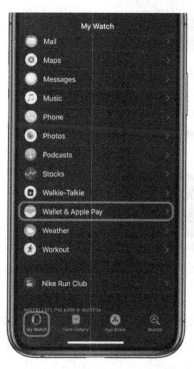

Pay for an item in a store with your smartwatch

❖ Press the side button twice quickly.
❖ Scroll to select one of the cards
❖ Take your smartwatch very close to the contactless card reader, with the screen facing the reader.

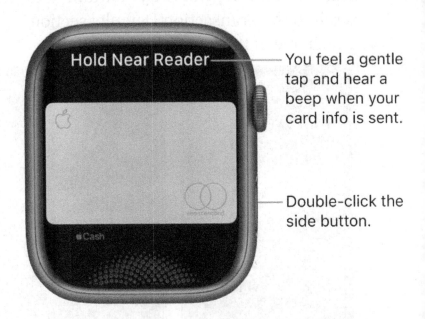

Hold Near Reader —————— You feel a gentle tap and hear a beep when your card info is sent.

————— Double-click the side button.

You'll feel a gentle tap & hear a beep to confirm that the payment info has been sent. You'll be notified when the transaction is confirmed.

Make in-app purchases

❖ When purchasing items in an application on your smartwatch, select the Apple Pay option during checkout.
❖ Go through the payment details, and press the side button twice quickly to make payments with your smartwatch.

WORKOUT

The Workout application provides tools to manage each workout.

Start a workout

❖ Launch the Workout application 🏃 on your smartwatch.
❖ Rotate the Digital Crown to one of the available workouts.

Touch the **Add Workout** button in the lower part of your display to show workouts like surfing or kickboxing.

❖ Touch the workout when you are ready to start.

Tap to set workout goals.

Turn the Digital Crown to choose another workout.

Pause & resume a workout

Press the Digital Crown & the side button simultaneously to pause a workout. Or, swipe right on the workout screen, and then touch the

Pause button. Touch the **Resume** button to continue the workout.

Begin an outdoor push wheelchair workout

If you specified that you use a wheelchair, you can begin an outdoor push exercise. Your smartwatch will track pushes instead of steps, and you can select the pace too.

Set your wheelchair status to health information

- ❖ Enter the Watch application on your phone.
- ❖ Click on the **My Watch** button, click on the **Health** button, and then click on Health Details.
- ❖ Click on the **Edit** button, click Wheelchair, and click Yes.
- ❖ When you are done, click on the **Done** button.

Begin an outdoor push exercise

- ❖ Enter the Workout application
- ❖ Rotate the Digital Crown to Outdoor Push Walking Pace or Outdoor Push Running Pace.
- ❖ Touch the workout when you are ready to start.

Adjust your smartwatch while working out

You can carry out any of the below while working out:

❖ See the progress you've made: Lift your hand to view your workout statistics, which include your heart rate, calories burned, distance covered, and more. Rotate the Digital Crown to check out more workout views, like Elevation, & Power.

❖ Play music while working out: While working out, swipe to the left to enter the Now Playing screen, from there you can select music & control the volume of the connected headphones. To select a playlist that'll automatically start playing when you start a workout, enter the Watch application on your phone, then touch the **My Watch** tab. Touch the **Workout** button, touch Workout Playlist, and then select one of the playlists.

Change workout views while working out

Begin a workout, and then rotate the Digital Crown to cycle through the workout views.

Use gym equipment with your smartwatch

Your smartwatch can pair & synchronize data with compatible cardio equipment like indoor bikes, elliptical, treadmills, & more, giving you more accurate workout data.

❖ First, check if your smartwatch is compatible with the gym equipment—you will see "Connects to Apple Watch" on the gym equipment.

❖ Ensure your smartwatch is set to detect gym equipment—head over to the Settings application, click on the **Workout** button, and then enable the **Detect Gym Equipment** feature.

❖ Take your smartwatch very close to the contactless reader on the equipment, and ensure the screen is facing the reader.
You'll feel a soft tap & hear a beep when your device pairs with the gym equipment.

❖ Press the Start button on the gym equipment to start the workout. Press the Stop button when you want to end the workout session.

End your workout

Your smartwatch will play a sound & vibrate when you reach your goal. If you still want to continue the workout, go ahead — your smartwatch will keep collecting data till you tell it to stop. When you are ready to end the workout:

❖ Swipe to the right, touch the **End** button, and then touch the **End Workout** button.

❖ Rotate the Digital Crown to scroll through the workout summary, then touch the **Done** button.

Review your workout history

❖ Enter the Fitness application on your phone.
❖ Click on the **Show More** button beside History, and then touch one of the workouts.

The summary includes exercise details, route, heartrate, & splits. You can view more details about each item by clicking the Show More button beside the item.

To see route summary you need to activate route tracking. Do any of the below to activate route tracking:

❖ Enter the Settings application on your smartwatch, head over to Privacy and Security> Location Service, touch Apple Watch Workout, and then touch the **While Using the App** option
❖ Enter the Settings application on your phone, head over to Privacy and Security> Location Service, touch Apple Watch Workout, and then touch the **While Using the App** option

Change your workout goals

❖ Enter the Workout application.
❖ Rotate the Digital Crown to go to the workout you want.
❖ Click on the More Options icon, and then click the **Create Workout** button.
❖ Touch a goal, like Time, Distance, or Calories; select a value; and then click on the **Done** button.

❖ Click on the modified goal to start the workout. Or, click on the Back button to save the modified workout, and then click on the workout when you are ready to start.

To delete an edited goal from a workout, go to the workout, click the More Options icon , click the Edit icon beside the edited goal, scroll down, click on the **Delete Workout** button, and then click on the **Delete** button.

Combine several activities into one workout

❖ Enter the Workout application.

❖ Start the 1ˢᵗ exercise—for instance an outdoor run.

❖ When you are ready to begin another exercise—such as outdoor cycling—simply swipe to the right, touch the **End** button, touch the **New Workout** button, and then select the workout.

❖ When you're done with all your activities, swipe to the right, touch the **End** button, and then touch the **End Workout** button.

❖ Rotate the Digital Crown to go through your workout results summary.

❖ Scroll down and then click on the **Done** button to save the workout.

Create a multisport workout

You can combine swimming, outdoor running, & cycling workouts in a Multisport Workout, and your smartwatch will automatically know when you switch between them.

- ❖ Enter the Workout application.
- ❖ Carry out any of the below:
  - ➢ If this is the first time you are using the multisport workout feature: Touch the Multisport workout, and then touch the **Create Workout** button.
  - ➢ If you have done a multisport workout before: Click on the More Options icon ⬤, then click on the **Create Workout** button.
- ❖ Click the **Add** button, and then click one of the activities—like, Outdoor Run.
- ❖ Keep adding activities by clicking on the Add button for each activity you want.
- ❖ Touch Untitled under Custom Tile, and then give the workout a name.
- ❖ After adding all the activities, touch the **Create Workout** button to store the workout.
- ❖ When you are ready to start a multisport workout, enter the Workout application, scroll to the Multisport workout, touch the More Options icon ⬤, and then touch one of the workouts.

To remove a Multisport workout from your device, click on the More Options icon ⬤ on the

Multisport workout tab, touch the Edit icon ⊘ beside the workout you plan on deleting, scroll down, touch the **Delete Workout** button, and then click on the **Delete** button.

Start a swimming workout

❖ Enter the Workout application.
❖ Rotate the Digital Crown to Pool Swim or Open Water Swim.
   For Pool Swim, set the length of the pool, and then touch the **Start** button
❖ When you are done, long-press the Digital Crown to unlock your smartwatch, touch the **End** button, and then touch the **End Workout** button.

Manually clear water from your smartwatch after swimming

When you begin a swim workout, your smartwatch will lock the screen with the Water Lock feature to prevent accidental taps. When you are out of the water, long-press the Digital Crown to unlock your display and clear water from your watch's speaker

❖ After swimming, press your watch's side button to enter the Controls Centre, and then touch the Water Lock button ⬤.

❖ Long-press the Digital Crown to unlock your display and clear water from your watch's speaker.

Update your weight & height

❖ Enter the Watch application on your phone.
❖ Touch the **My Watch** button, head over to Health> Health Detail, and then click on the **Edit** button.
❖ Touch Weight or Height, and then make the changes.

Change the measurement unit

You can change the measurement unit the Workout application uses.

❖ Launch the Settings application.
❖ Click on the **Workout** button, scroll, and then click on Unit of Measure.

Automatically pause cycling & running workouts

❖ Enter the Settings application on your smartwatch.
❖ Click on the **Workout** button, click on Auto-Pause, and then enable the **Auto-Pause** feature.

Your watch will automatically pause & resume cycling & running workouts—for example, if you stop to drink water or cross the road.

Activate workout reminders

For running, walking, & other exercises, your smartwatch detects when you are moving and prompts you to start the Workout application. It'll still remind you to end the exercise when you stop. Adhere to the directives on your display to activate or disable workout reminders.

* ❖ Enter the Settings application on your smartwatch.
* ❖ Click on the **Workout** button, and then change the End Workout Reminders & Start Workout Reminders setting.

Save power while working out

You can extend the battery life of your smartwatch while exercising.

* ❖ Enter the Settings application on your smartwatch.
* ❖ Click on the **Workout** button, and then enable **Low Power Mode**.

INDEX

A

B

C

Made in the USA
Las Vegas, NV
14 November 2024

11820667R00213